M000315114

From
Russia
with
Lev

FRED RAGSDALE

Copyright © 2016 Fred Ragsdale
All rights reserved
First Edition

Fulton Books, Inc.
Meadville, PA

Published by Fulton Books 2016

ISBN 978-1-63338-292-3 (Paperback)
ISBN 978-1-63338-293-0 (Digital)

Printed in the United States of America

Contents

Acknowledgments

This book is dedicated, with love to Jeanne Butler-Smith.

God certainly used Jeanne in a wonderful way to help facilitate the adoption of Lev. She constantly communicated with me the conditions, not only at the children's home but also the condition in which she found Lev. She would take my letters to Lev and send his letters to me after they were translated by Pasha Baranov. As a long-term registered nurse missionary from the United States to Russia, Jeanne has a great knowledge of the country and its people. Her ability to speak Russian was also very helpful to the teams that went to the region multiple times. Jeanne was a blessing to me and to Lev.

Also, my sincerest thanks to the following:

Pastor Stephen Hess—His help in editing the manuscript and his many suggestions for improvement have yielded a far better book than what was initially scripted. I want to thank Stephen for being not only a brother in the Lord but a true and very loyal friend.

Pasha Baranov—His help was invaluable during our visits to Russia. Pasha always joined our teams and assisted in translating for the team members. Pasha, who is the current pastor of Calvary Chapel, Vladimir, consistently e-mailed me and others about the situation in his country. I thank him for translating many of the letters between Lev and myself. Thank you, Pasha, for all you did for us.

Dmitry (Dima) Nikitin—A true brother in the Lord, Dima served the team from the US on all our trips. He also led worship and taught the children songs and Bible stories. He was a young brother with a very big heart and a great sense of humor. He will certainly receive a reward one day in the kingdom for all he did for the children of Lyahi.

Lena Shagin-Rayeva—Without her taking me around Vladimir after the court hearing and translating for me while we made the rounds of official offices to pick up various documents, I don't know how it would have been done. Lena also helped Lev sell his flat in Vladimir. Thank you, Lena, from the bottom of my heart.

Danny Hodges—Pastor of Calvary Chapel, St. Petersburg, who allowed the teams to go unhindered to Russia multiple times. So much of what was accomplished in Russia is due to the love that Danny had for the Russian people.

Finally, thanks to all the team members, both Russian and American, who were absolutely wonderful in their dedication to the children of the orphanages. It was a true blessing to travel with them, to worship with them, and to work with them as we brought the knowledge of the Lord to the children of Lyahi.

Long term missionary to Russia, Jeanne Beckner-Smith

Introduction

During most of my life, I have always felt the need to be in control of my circumstances. I believed that I should be able to determine where my life was heading at any given time. To have circumstances arise in my life that I neither understood nor felt I could control was alien to me. However, I have learned since 1997 that I can neither predict what is going to happen in my life nor control things that do happen. It was in 1997 that my wife decided to end our twenty-eight-year marriage. I think we were both tired of pretending that everything was okay when it wasn't. Religious differences had become almost intolerable, and many of the traditions that we had previously shared became nonexistent.

Divorce is a very traumatic event, even when it appears justified. I don't think many people walk away from a divorce unscathed, especially when it is from a long-term marriage. Oftentimes, some of the damage is fractured relations with children of that marriage. It was because of a damaged relationship with my son that I prayed for God to give me another son. I wasn't sure my relationship with my son, who was no longer speaking with me, would be repaired. I can understand what some readers may be thinking, especially those who subscribe to the biblical view that marriage is forever and the vows taken should not be broken no matter the circumstances. I understand that. I subscribed to that. However, we live in a broken world of which I am a part of. When I married, I had no intention of ever divorcing. I took my vows seriously, and no matter what was happening, it was not my desire to divorce my wife and cause anger in my son. It was my wife who decided to file for divorce although I share in the blame. I can imagine that some readers will not understand God answering a prayer for another son from someone like me. I can only say that I'm glad God is not as harsh as some people are in their judgment. I believe my sin of divorce was forgiven at the cross and that God loves me as much now as he did prior to the divorce.

God answered my prayer in an extremely unorthodox way as he often does. I could never in a million years have conceived of the path that God had in store for me. I still marvel to this day at how God worked in my life to fulfill his plan to answer my prayer and to give me another son. It was a roller-coaster ride that I will never forget. Every time I have shared this story, people often tell me I need to write a book. Giving this story in church, I have seen people reduced to tears. People have come up to me years later to tell me how the story impacted their lives. If God had told me beforehand what he was going to do and how he would do it, I would have backed out and told him "no, thanks." God's plan unfolded over five years and at times had me on my knees crying out to him and at other times doubting whether it was even God's plan or maybe just my own selfish desires. I have been to Russia ten times. That's amazing in itself as there was never a time in my life when I wanted to go to Russia. How God got me to go the first time was simply amazing and could only have come from the hand of God.

Hopefully, as you read this book, you will come to a realization that no matter how difficult a desire of your heart may seem, if it is God's will, he can make it come to pass. As stated in 1 John 5:14, "This is the confidence we have in approaching God: that if we ask anything according to his will, he hears us" and in Luke 1:37, "For nothing is impossible with God." One thing I have learned is to never doubt God's ability to answer a prayer even when we can't figure out how he could do it. Once I started down the path God set me on, I was at times full of doubt and disillusionment. You will see that I could never take anything for granted, that I could never think that everything was going to work out, and that I could never have confidence in my own ability but would have to depend completely on God. God could have made my journey easy. The two plans I had chosen for God were: he could give me a new wife who had an adoptable son right here in St. Petersburg or I could marry and father a child. But my plans were not his plans. So why did I have to go through so much? I believe it was for you. It was for you to know that if God would do this for me, your desires can also come to pass. He won't always make it easy, and many times you will wonder what he is up to or why he is taking so long. That's okay. Just don't ever think that he is incapable of fulfilling your desires. God doesn't telegraph his plans to us. He doesn't give us a script ahead of time. He works them out in and through us. The great men of the Bible had no idea what God was doing in their lives most of the time, but they had faith to trust him and go where he led them. Whenever I was ready to throw in the towel and give up, I remembered the faith of Daniel, Joseph, David, and many other heroes of the faith and knew that until the Lord finally spoke to tell me it was over, I must carry on. In essence, the story you will read in this book is about faith—faith that God will finish what he has started. I have heard it said many times that God always answers sincere prayers. Sometimes the answer is yes, sometimes no, and sometimes wait. Yes and no are easy to understand; but it is the times when we must wait that are the most difficult. I would say to readers, if you have asked God for his favor in a situation and he tells you to wait, just wait. It is very probable that he is preparing you to receive the blessing. God had to prepare me to receive his blessing. I no longer doubt what God can do for those who seek his favor. I once met a young Christian man who told me he had been on the verge of committing suicide because of severe health and emotional problems. However, he said he never did because he was afraid that God would answer his prayers for healing the day after if he had just waited. He didn't want to miss out on what God would do in his life. Today, even though some problems are still there, he has a joy that he had never experienced before, and he is truly happy.

Through this journey, I have a deeper faith than I could have ever had otherwise. It was an extraordinarily difficult journey, one that I would not want to repeat, but I know that God lives and that he rewards those who seek him. The people he put into my life at just the right times to help me, to reassure me, to love me, to encourage me, and to love Lev had to come from his hand. To me, there is no other answer. Not luck, not coincidence, not being in the right place at the right time. No, it was one hundred percent favor from God.

May you be blessed as you read this book.

CHAPTER 1

The Divorce and First Mission Trip

It was 1996, and a beautiful December day in Florida, when my wife of twenty-seven years announced that she wanted a divorce. Our marriage in the last year had been very difficult. We had major differences, primarily in our religious beliefs. Although I didn't regularly attend church when we first married, I considered myself a Christian. I thought she was also; however, early in our marriage, she had become a Jehovah's Witness. When we married in 1968, I believed her to be a lifelong Methodist, especially since she had been the secretary to the pastor at her family's home church in Philadelphia where we both grew up. During our courtship and engagement, she never mentioned to me her interest in the Jehovah's Witnesses religion. When she eventually revealed to me, after we were married in the Methodist church, I was very upset and disappointed. I admit I knew very little about the Jehovah's Witnesses. All I could picture in my mind was my wife standing out on some street corner peddling *Watchtower* and *Awake* periodicals or going door to door annoying people on Sunday mornings. Eventually, I started studying the Bible with some friends and attending church. I wanted to find out for myself if what she was saying was true. The more I studied the Bible, the more I found fault with her new beliefs. Neither of us could convince each other of the rightness of our very different positions. She felt just as strongly in what she believed as I did and had no interest in hearing my arguments. We went for about fifteen years generally ignoring the topic of religion. Just like other long-term marriages, we had our good times, some very good, and our bad times. The bad times occurred mostly when the topic of religion periodically reared its ugly head. On the outside, we looked like a perfect family: mother, father, and son. However, on the inside, there was serious trouble brewing.

I tried to understand what the Witnesses stood for, even attending their services and reading their *Watchtower* and *Awake* periodicals. As hard as I might try, I could not reconcile their beliefs with what I felt to be the truth of scripture. My wife and I had many arguments over what the Bible said and meant. We tried marriage counseling by both secular and religious counselors. The secular counselor said that there was a gulf between us that no bridge could span. Jehovah's Witnesses do not celebrate holidays. I hated the inability to celebrate holidays in my home: no Christmas, Thanksgiving, Easter, Valentine's Day, and no patriotic holidays such as the Fourth of July or Memorial Day. Also, Jehovah's Witnesses are not permitted to vote. As the years went by, my resentment grew. I'm sure I was no angel to live with during that time. We survived by ignoring our religious differences. During this time, I prayed that my wife would come to know the Lord as I did. I'm sure she was praying that I would come into her faith. I knew deep in my heart that at some time, we would both have to face the truth and either decide that our spiritual differences were not that important, one of us would join the other's religion, or we would end up going our separate ways. I also knew deep in my heart that I would never initiate a divorce. I believed that no matter how difficult the road, I was married for life. I never wanted to be a divorced man, and I didn't want our son to go through that either. Looking back, I realized that was not a very smart decision. I know that our marriage ended many years before our divorce. We were living unequally yoked in a pretend life and a pretend marriage.

At the time of the divorce, our son, Christopher, was an adult who was very close to me and his mother; I knew that divorce would be devastating to his image of us and himself. Once he was told of the decision, he was, as I suspected, broken by the news. Even though Christopher had grown up attending services at the Kingdom Hall of Jehovah's Witnesses, I refused to allow him to be baptized as a Witness until he was eighteen years old and could make the decision on his own. Baptism is what brings you officially into the religion. By the time he was eighteen, he had decided for himself that he did not want to be baptized and stopped attending their services on a regular basis. However, his indoctrination to their beliefs was still strong, and I could sense that he supported his mother during this time. I made a pointed effort not to involve him in the struggle by not speaking ill of his mother or the decision that she had made. I could sense him distancing himself from me, which was very hurtful since he was the only living child we had. Our first child, Susan, died several days after birth due to a birth defect. The more I tried to draw close to him, the further he distanced himself from me to the point that we could barely have a conversation of more than three words. He got a job in Tampa and moved there. I would call him and ask what I had done to him, and I would never get an answer. He would just say things like "I don't want to talk about it" and hang up.

Peggy and I decided that we would get an amicable no-fault divorce, without argument or the hiring of attorneys, which is quite possible in Florida. Sometime during the early part of 1997, my wife did hire an attorney. I stuck by my word and did not. That decision came back to haunt me later as I did not know just how vicious divorce attorneys could be. Just to set the record straight, during our marriage, I always supported my family. We lived in very nice homes in stable neighborhoods, both in Pennsylvania and also in Florida where we had moved in 1991. Our home in Florida was purchased new. I truly expected to live the rest of my life in that home. But it was not to be.

We moved into separate bedrooms as we awaited the sale of our home. I stayed in the guest room, and she stayed in the master bedroom. We were civil to each other if not exactly cordial. It's always amazing to me that when love is gone from a home, you can hate the house you once loved. I could not wait to get as far away from it as possible.

In the spring of 1997, as we waited for the court case to proceed, I decided to go on a short-term mission trip with my church. I had never in my life wanted to go on a mission trip, especially not to Russia. However, during a men's conference, I heard a missionary, Pastor Mark Coppel, who had been serving in Russia, speak of the great need of people in foreign lands to hear the good news of the gospel and that it was up to us to bring them that news. Russia had just come out of seventy years of official atheism, and biblical knowledge there was very low as it was in many countries. His message moved me, and I decided right then and there that I would go on the very next mission trip (not to Russia though) that was announced by the church. The church I attended, Calvary Chapel of St. Petersburg, sponsored many mission trips throughout the world, and I looked forward to going to a nice, warm, pleasant place like the Carribean or South America. As providence would have it, the very next trip announced was to Russia. I decided I would keep my vow, so I signed up for the trip. However, there was one major problem. The trip would cost each person one thousand four hundred dollars, and I didn't have the money to spare for such a trip since preparing for the divorce and trying to find a place to live had left me with few expendable funds. I simply couldn't afford to go on this trip unless God provided. I talked to the mission pastor, Vivian Laird, and told him of my situation. I also told him that I didn't want to ask anyone for money as short-term missionaries usually do (pride, I suppose). He related to me that he was a long-term missionary in Africa for over thirty years and only once asked for support. He said that God always supplied what he needed. He also told me that if it was God's will that I go to Russia, God would see that I had the money. That was somewhat reassuring because if God didn't supply the money, then I would be off the hook and could wait for a less expensive and more pleasant trip to come around, such as the Bahamas.

For some really strange reason, which I couldn't identify at the time, I felt that God wanted me in Russia. But I knew it would take a miracle for me to get the money in time for the trip especially since I had no intention of asking anyone for support. The following Sunday, I came to church, and as I was walking into the auditorium, the brother who worked in the sound booth, Lang, spoke to me. We greeted each other. Then strangely, he asked me if I was going on the Russia trip. I said that I planned to; then he responded that he would like to help support me financially. He pulled out his checkbook and wrote a check for seven hundred dollars. I couldn't believe it. I knew this brother only as an acquaintance, and here he was writing a check for half of the cost of the trip. How did he know? I hadn't shared my desire with anyone other than the pastor. I could barely wait until the service was over so I could go and find Pastor Laird and tell him what happened. After the service, I found him in the courtyard of the church, and I shared the good news with him. While I was talking to him, another woman, Elizabeth, whom I didn't know at all, came over to speak to the pastor. The pastor introduced me to her, and without anyone saying anything, she also asked me if I was planning to go to Russia. I looked at my shirt to see if there was a sign pinned on me saying, "I want to go to Russia." She then said that she would like to help support my trip and wrote a check for three hundred fifty dollars. I was shell-shocked. By the following Sunday, I was informed by the church office that my entire trip (one thousand four hundred dollars) was paid for. In one week without my asking anyone for anything, God supplied all the funds, and I was the first person to raise all their funds. All I now needed was spending money. The missions' pastor said that God must really want me in Russia. I began to wonder why. What did I have to contribute? I felt that I was going as much to escape from the pressures of the pending divorce as to bring the gospel to Russia. I had learned not to question why God does what he does.

It was July 1997, when our team left Tampa en route to St. Petersburg, Russia. It was a long tiring overnight flight with a change of planes in Helsinki, Finland, and then on to St. Petersburg. Our team of fourteen was dragging by the time we got through immigration control, baggage claim, and on to the hotel. Many of the people who attended Calvary Chapel, St. Petersburg, Russia, met us at the airport and rode back to the hotel with us.

The young guys and gals who would serve as our translators were part of this church. They were really awesome folks, mostly in their teens, and they spoke very good English, which was wonderful since we spoke very little Russian. We had been taught some important phrases to know before we left Florida; but mostly, we were very dependent on these young folks. The ride from the airport through the streets of St. Petersburg was eye-opening for me and all the others on the trip. I had never seen such historical-looking buildings even though I eventually learned that St. Petersburg was not an especially ancient city as many others in Russia were. The churches and cathedrals were amazing, but most of the buildings looked like they were in various states of disrepair. As tired as I was, I couldn't help but look at the sights out the bus window. The hotel wasn't bad, but not great either. The hardest thing for us was that mosquitoes (huge ones) were a major problem during the summer in northern Russia and hotel windows did not have screens. We would spend half the night killing mosquitoes so we could get some sleep. Also, it didn't get dark until one or two in the morning, and the sun was coming back up by four o'clock in the morning.

One of the concerns that I didn't mention to my teammates was the fact that I was the only person of color on our team. I knew that that there were not many persons of color in Russia, and I was worried that I may be mistreated or ignored. I didn't want to lay that concern on my teammates, but it was there in the gut of my stomach. Persons of color are always aware of their circumstances when they are among primarily Caucasian groups. I was continually looking out the window of the bus to see if I saw any persons of color in the city. I didn't. Thankfully, the young Christians from the Russian church treated me with as much kindness as they did all the others. I was still concerned about how I would be treated once we started our street ministry within the general public. Growing up during the worst of the cold war, I had a slight fear of Russia. I wasn't comfortable going to a land that we were taught to fear as children.

Everyone on our team had a specific assignment. We were either part of the drama team, the small band, or working with puppets. Our plan was to minister on the streets of St. Petersburg in front of metro stations where huge numbers of people would pass. We would hand out Bibles, tracts, and invitations to evening services in a theater we had rented. It was very hot during the two weeks we were there, and we were all exhausted at the end of each day. It was a long walk from our hotel to the metro station. It was late at night by the time we returned to our hotel, and since it was the time of the year for the midnight sun, it didn't get dark until after midnight. We had to get up early each morning to start the process all over again. Most people would take our literature and Bibles, but only a few would stop and talk, and when they did, we would have to call over one of the translators to help us. My concerns about my treatment amid the general public evaporated once I had spent time on the streets. People seemed to pay no more attention to me than they did to any of the others. I still hadn't seen any other persons of color.

Everybody coming out of the metro station seemed to be in a big hurry. Anyone who has visited St. Petersburg and rode their subway system is always amazed at how deep the stations are in the ground. They are deeper than any subway system in the world. Some stations are two hundred eighty-two feet below street level, and riding the escalator down to the tracks is an experience. The escalators move rapidly, probably twice as fast as American escalators, and you can barely see the bottom of the stairs because they are so far down. It is important to stand to the right as there are folks running down the left side of the stairs. It is such a long ride to the bottom that you see folks sitting on the stairs reading a book. At the bottom is an employee with a control lever who can stop the stairs if someone falls down, which I understand happens frequently. The stations themselves were absolutely beautiful. They were nothing like the disasters of American subway stations. The subway systems in New York City, Philadelphia, and Chicago are shameful in comparison. Even the Washington DC system pales in comparison to the St. Petersburg system. The stations in St. Petersburg were mostly marble with fine paintings and chandeliers. You could not see the trains arrive as the platforms are sealed from the tracks, which means the stations are unusually quiet. When a train arrives, doors along the platform open in conjunction with the subway doors, and you can enter. In no way could someone fall or be pushed onto the tracks.

At the end of our day in front of the metro stations, we would have dinner and then head over to the theater where we would always get a small crowd. Many parents brought their kids to see the puppets and to hear the band, not so much to hear the message of salvation.

I was on the drama team. The dramas were all without words and could easily be understood by the audience. We spent two very hot weeks doing this. The temperatures were in the high eighties or low nineties each day, and there was no air-conditioning. On Saturday, after the first week, we went sightseeing. I was totally blown away by the awesome Hermitage Museum, which was the palace of the Russian czars. It houses the second largest art collection in the world behind the Louvre in Paris. All I can say is it was staggeringly beautiful with more art than I could take in if I spent a month there. The czar's throne room was worth the price of admission all by itself. Never have I seen so much crimson and gold plating.

By the time we left Russia, I didn't know whether I or our team had made a difference. We did make friends with many young Russian Christians who served as our interpreters. I loved St. Petersburg, which is a beautiful city, and the people we talked to were quite warm and open. I was somewhat surprised at the number of people (generally young) who could speak English. I found out that all Russian students must take either English or German as one of their foreign languages starting in elementary school. They were awfully pleasant to converse with, and they shared much about their lives in Russia. Most churches we saw were Russian Orthodox, and generally only elderly people attended them. Younger Christians said the Orthodox Church lives in the past and didn't seem to care that the young didn't attend. In Russia, the Orthodox Church is not supported by donations from those who attend but is supported by the government. Therefore, the priests who are on the government's payroll must do as the government says. Priests do not have the freedom to say what they want and are prohibited from criticizing the government policies. There are other churches, but they are generally quite small and are supported by tithes and offerings. The church we were working with (Calvary Chapel, St. Petersburg) had a congregation of about forty or fifty people, but they were very much on fire for the Lord. They had a freedom that the Orthodox churches did not. When I came back home, I was so grateful for the experience, and it certainly took my mind off the divorce action. I still wasn't sure why God made it so easy for me to go to Russia. Was it just to forget about my current circumstances or was there something more meaningful in store for me?

We finally sold the house in Palm Harbor, and I moved out into a small condo on St. Pete Beach that I rented from a friend. I was now living just one block from the beach and the Gulf of Mexico. It was a taste of heaven. Except for my working at St. Petersburg College, it was like being on a perpetual vacation. Most evenings, I would go to the beach and take a book to read until the sun went down. What spectacular sunsets there are over the gulf. As I waited for our day in court, I kept asking God what I was going to do with the rest of my life. By now, my son was not speaking to me at all. I would call, and as soon as he heard my voice, he would hang up the phone. I felt terribly alone. Friends that we had made as a couple seemed to disappear. My family stood by me, but they were all in Pennsylvania. My mother, especially, kept in regular contact. To her credit, she never said negative things about my wife. She was just very sorry that we were divorcing after so many years. She would encourage me to keep praying and reading my Bible to see what God had in store for me.

Our day in court finally arrived in October 1997. I won't burden you with the details, but I did not fare very well. My wife's lawyer took extreme advantage in that I was representing myself. He lied and completely fabricated stories to the judge. I felt like a complete idiot standing there realizing that I was going to get smashed like a bug. Because I had spent twenty-four years as a police officer and detective, I had been on the witness stand many, many times in my career. However, in divorce court, unlike criminal court, very little proof of allegations is required. It just depends on the judge you get. My wife got everything she wanted including alimony for life. I was unable to introduce evidence I had that showed she didn't need alimony because she had a good income from a business she owned and operated. I was given all the bills, with the exception of a car she purchased during our time of estrangement. Although there was no child to support, she was given over a thousand dollars a month in alimony. I almost died. I asked the judge how long the alimony would continue, since I knew that in my former state of Pennsylvania, alimony only lasted three years unless the spouse was unable to ever earn a living. The judge told me that it would be for life. My income at the college was in the midthirties. Thirteen thousand dollars a year in alimony seemed impossible on my salary. How could I pay her and live? I walked out of the courtroom stunned. Anger was boiling up inside me, and when I saw her lawyer in the hallway, I gave him a serious piece of my mind. I asked him how he in good conscience could lie like he did. He listened to me but never said a word. I supposed he was used to husbands saying that to him.

I walked outside to my car. I remember it was a beautiful sunny day in Clearwater. I sat in my car, turned the air conditioner on, and with tears in my eyes, I prayed. I told God that I didn't understand all that had happened, but I knew somehow, someday, it would all make sense. I told him I didn't want to live my life in anger, and I wanted to live in peace with my former wife, my son, and even the attorney. For some strange reason, I remember specifically asking God for a new son. I guess I was so devastated at losing my marriage and my son that I think I felt that if I had a new son, it would somehow make up for the loss. I felt God saying to me something about restoring what the locust had eaten. I knew that what I was hearing from God was somewhere in the Bible, and I just had to find it. When I got home, I got out my concordance and looked up the words locust. I found the passage in the Book of Joel. In Joel 2:25, it says, "I will repay you for the years the locusts have eaten." I knew that this was the verse God had given me to hold on to. I felt that it was a promise to me from

God, and I wasn't about to let it go. God spoke to me in my car, and I knew that I was no longer alone. My anger was completely gone. That moment of God reassuring me was the most important part of the whole divorce proceeding. I felt closer to him than ever.

Sometimes when we are going through troubling times, we wonder if God is paying any attention to our plight. Does he hear our prayers? We wonder if we are being punished for some sin or if God simply doesn't care. Deep down, I know these thoughts aren't true; however, when you are in the middle of trouble, all sorts of thoughts come into your mind. In hindsight, I realize that they were irrational thoughts and that God is never unconcerned about his people. God used everything that I experienced to bring me to the final result that he had planned from the beginning. Did God plan for my divorce? No, God wants marriages not only to survive but to thrive. I think the more important question is: was this marriage in God's plan for me? During my courtship years, I was estranged from the church. I didn't want anything to do with organized religion or religious people even though I maintained my belief in God. I just wanted to get married and be like my friends. God has given all of us free will. Even though he does not cause tragedies in our lives, he can subsequently use them for our good. As the highest of God's creatures, we have been given a wonderful gift: the gift of free choice. I once heard a pastor say in a sermon, "We have never committed a sin that we didn't choose to commit." Once we can accept that, we can then stop the blame game and put the responsibility for our sins and bad choices correctly on our own shoulders. I chose to marry even though there were some troubling signs in the pit of my stomach that warned me to wait. She was a fine upstanding woman, but maybe she wasn't the right woman for me. Adam and Eve chose to eat the fruit from the tree forbidden by God. Yes, they were tempted, but it was their own desires that eventually caused them to make the bad choice to eat the fruit. That's why God judged them. If the serpent had forced the fruit down their throats against their will, there would have been no judgment of Adam and Eve. They would still have been in a state of innocence. What we can glean from the scripture is that they had the ability to disobey God, but they were not forced to. It appears that the only sin they could have committed at that time was to eat from the Tree of the Knowledge of Good and Evil.

So if sin is a choice, why do we choose to sin, knowing the consequences are always displeasing to God? Probably for the same reasons that Adam and Eve sinned; it appears to satisfy our flesh more than obedience to God. But God, knowing that after sin was introduced into the world that man would continue to sin and be separated from him, had a wonderful plan in place. He sent his son Jesus to provide the redemption that only he could provide.

Leaving the courthouse after my divorce, I went back to my apartment very disillusioned and sad. I was trying desperately to make sense of what happened just now and over the previous year. I never want to leave the impression that my marriage dissolved simply because of my spouse and her becoming a Jehovah's Witness. It would be a rare thing for one person to be one hundred percent responsible for the dissolution of a marriage. If my former spouse were writing a book, I'm sure she could legitimately point out many of my short-comings, and she would be correct. In a marriage that lasts for over twenty-eight years, both partners at times do things that disturb the other partner to a major degree. I also can look back on many fun times and years of reasonably stress-free living. We enjoyed family vacations, which many times took us to the Caribbean, Florida, or Canada. We tried on our wedding anniversaries to take a weekend away from our son and go to a bed and breakfast or quick trip to another locale. These usually included the Poconos, the Pennsylvania countryside, or New York City. On these trips, we truly enjoyed each other's company. I have always had the "travel bug" and loved the anticipation of the next trip.

As I tried to analyze my life, I knew that nothing would ever be the same. I would never live in the nice homes we shared, take trips as a family, enjoy Sunday cookouts, or even have fun with the same couples we had come to know and love. That life was over. What do I do now? Even my closest friends seemed somewhat distant as I was unable to truly share with them what was going on in my heart. For the first time in my life, I felt loneliness. Prior to this time, even if I was alone, I didn't feel lonely. I cried out to God to please bring someone into my life as a companion. (Many therapists warn against quickly getting into a new relationship right after a divorce. I think that many folks are just longing for what was, not thinking about what could be.) I would go to church, and when people would ask me how I was doing, I would always reply, "I'm doing fine." I couldn't bring myself to open up. Everybody at church seemed so happy and without cares (at least in my mind). I missed the stability of married life even when things weren't going well. I missed my son. I wanted desperately to replace what was lost. Publicly, I was trying to be stoic, but privately, I was dying a little bit at a time. When I would see happy families in church, I would envy them. I even looked for single mothers at church, possibly believing that I could remarry and gain a son or a family. That didn't work out too well as most of the single moms I met had their own serious life issues. After twenty-eight years, I was not used to being a single man. I didn't know how single men acted or what was expected of me. Should I start dating? Should I join a singles group? Should I let it be known that I am now available? Should I go to places where singles hang out? I didn't even know where those places were. I think if I were still living in Pennsylvania, it would have been easier because most of my longtime friends and all my family were there. I would have felt freer to open up and confide in folks. Living in Florida, it was different. I hadn't known folks as long. I did have one really good friend in Florida. Cezar and I had been co-workers at the college, and that developed into a great friendship. Although there was a significant age difference between us, we seemed to really get along and understand each other. To this day, he probably doesn't understand how much he helped me get through the mess I was in. While married, my wife seemed quite envious of Cezar, and I never understood why. Cezar and I are still friends to this day, and it was an honor to be best man at his wedding. He is currently a pilot in the US Air Force and has had quite a few tours to the Middle East.

In retrospect, it is easy to see how God was working in my life, but at the time, it was extremely difficult to see. There were days when I felt that God had abandoned me or was going to leave me in my mess. I continued to faithfully attend church services and to do volunteer work when I could. Friends that I had at church were quite good to me and helped me to overcome the situation I was in.

The year after my divorce, I started to recover financially and wanted to move out of the small apartment and hopefully into a house of my own. I stayed in the apartment for one year, but during that year, I looked, with the help of a real estate agent, for a house. The problem I had was that I could not seem to accumulate a decent down payment plus closing costs during the year. The agent told me that we should look for homes that I could afford to pay monthly payments for and let him worry about the down payment and closing costs. Finally, I found a three-bedroom home in St. Petersburg. It needed a lot of work, but there were some really good points about the house. It was solid masonry with a brick exterior. There were two full bathrooms and a family room; however, the appliances were in extreme need of replacement. The house was fully carpeted with ugly shag carpeting that had a terrible odor. Because I am reasonably handy, I decided to go ahead and purchase the house knowing that I could make many of the improvements that needed to be made. But I was fearful that I would go to closing and be asked for thousands of dollars that I didn't have. The realtor assured me that I would be okay. We went through the closing, and not only did no one ask me for any money, they gave me a check for eight hundred fifty dollars. Why? To this day, I have not gone back to look at the paperwork to see why I was entitled to the money. However, I am convinced it was God helping me to be able to move and to do the initial updates and repairs.

Cezar came over prior to my moving in, and we pulled up all the shag carpet, took down the filthy draperies, and painted the entire house. We also rented a scrubbing machine and scrubbed the floors, which were terrazzo. When we finished, the house looked pretty good, and the awful smell that penetrated the house was gone. I was very happy to be moving in to my own home although I wondered why I needed a home with three bedrooms. After all, I was going to be the only one living there, wasn't I?

Second Mission Trip

January 2000

In 1999, the church announced another two-week mission trip to Russia—this time to Moscow in January of 2000. Although I had little desire to go back to Russia, especially in the dead of winter, I felt that it would be nice to see Moscow, since on my first trip, we had only gone to St. Petersburg. Strangely, I signed up to go on the trip. This time I had funds to go without needing help from others. Our purpose was to assist Russian pastors as they attended an annual one-week conference in Moscow. The pastors were from all over Russia. Some even spent over a week traveling by train, coming all the way from the East Coast of Russia on the Pacific. Compared with the first mission trip, this one was very easy and relaxed. We did everything we could to help the attendees enjoy the conference: we took care of their children, assisted with meals, gave out gifts, and encouraged them all.

Moscow was incredible. It was the largest city I had ever been in since it is larger than New York City. I expected it to be dull and gray; actually, it was the opposite. It was a very lively city with many shops and restaurants. Downtown Moscow at night is aglow with most of the buildings bathed in lighting. The streets are full of people walking, dining, and shopping. Going to Red Square was a real treat. It was so much larger than I imagined, and the walls of the Kremlin were gigantic. We got to see Lenin's tomb, the GUM department store, which is fabulous, the underground mall, and the changing of the guard at the Kremlin. St. Basil's Cathedral in Red Square is a gem and a must-see on any trip to Moscow. Sadly, it no longer serves as a church but as a museum.

At the end of the conference, our pastor, Danny, said that we would be going up to St. Petersburg by train so that he could preach at a Calvary Chapel there. We took an overnight train from Moscow to St. Petersburg; it was an exciting trip. I had never been on a train overnight, and it was a thrill to have a bed in one of the compartments. We spent some time in the dining car truly enjoying the trip. Lying in the bed and looking out the window as the train rumbled along through the different villages was really enjoyable. Everything was snow covered en route to St. Petersburg. We arrived in St. Petersburg on a cold, snowy Saturday morning. Danny said that we had a free day and wanted to know what we would like to do. He said that we would be going to the circus in the evening, but we had a whole day to do something else. He suggested we either go to a hospital to visit with patients or to an orphanage to visit orphans. Since most of us had been to a hospital but never to an orphanage, we all voted to go to an orphanage.

I had no idea what to expect when we arrived at the orphanage that afternoon. I was quite surprised that the building was very attractive and appeared to be in excellent condition. We were welcomed in by the orphanage director who escorted us into the large "day room." She had some of the children bring out drinks and pastries, which were very good. The director spoke English and explained how most of the children ended up in an orphanage. This was a state-run orphanage, as are most orphanages in Russia. She told us that many of the children in residence are not orphans in the traditional sense, where both parents are dead, but are social orphans. This means that their parents had chosen to give them up or the children were taken from them by the state because of physical abuse or parental addiction to drugs or alcohol. She was up-front about the fact that the orphanages needed funds and that they hoped that visitors, especially foreign visitors, would help them financially. She also stated that a number of the children were available for adoption; however, we weren't there to do either. Later during the visit, the children put on a show for us. I must say that they were very talented and appeared quite happy and healthy. Some children sang Russian songs for us; some danced, and some performed skits. It was a very entertaining afternoon. After the performances, the children came and socialized with us, the guests. Some could speak a little English, and all were very hospitable. It was a great afternoon, and we all felt we would like to spend more time there and, if possible, raise funds for the orphanage when we returned home. With a little sadness, we left and prepared to go to the circus. I won't speak on the circus because I was very disappointed. Russians are well-known for their circuses, but I found the trainers to be quite cruel to the animals, especially the bears. Suffice it to say, the acts we saw and the treatment of the animals would not have been tolerated in the US.

The next day, we went to the St. Petersburg Calvary Chapel, where Pastor Danny would be preaching. I saw old friends from my first trip to St. Petersburg in 1997. It was a great day and a lot of fun walking around that beautiful city again, although this time in the cold of January. The next day, it was time to return home to St. Petersburg, Florida.

When I got home, I was very excited about our experience on this trip. However, when people asked me about the highlights of the trip, it seemed that the highlight for me was not the pastor's conference but the visit to the orphanage. I was so impressed by the children, and I wondered if children in American orphanages were as delightful. At this point, I felt no need to ever return to Russia. I had toured St. Petersburg and Moscow and had no desire to go again. I really believed that would be my last time in Russia, although there was still a nagging thought deep in my spirit about why God ever provided for me to go to Russia in the first place. That still was not settled in my mind. As far as I was concerned, this was my second and final trip to Russia, and I still had no clue what God was up to.

CHAPTER 3

First Summer Camp in Lyahi, Russia

June 2000

Months later, there was an announcement of a third mission trip to Russia. This time, it would be to set up camps for orphans so they could get out of the orphanage for the summer. It would be to a little village six hours east of Moscow called Lyahi. The description of the trip was as follows:

> Deep in the Russian countryside, surrounded by beautiful birch forests, next to a lazy river, in the Melenki region, lies the village of Lyahi. Far from the bustle and city lights of Moscow and St. Petersburg, this village contains a regional orphanage comprised of boys and girls aged eight to sixteen. For these children, who have been deemed "learning disabled" and therefore dismissed by the state, this will be the best their life will get. Once leaving the orphanage

at age sixteen, they are on their own to fend for themselves. This usually leads to crime, drugs, prostitution, or worse. Up until now, the light of Christ has only dimly reached them. As Christians, we understand the impact a full knowledge of the love of Jesus can have on one's life.

As much as I did not desire to return to Russia again, I felt excited about this trip because it would be focused on orphans. My memory of the St. Petersburg orphanage was so vivid; I just had to go on this trip. I was really happy when my application was accepted, and I became a member of the team of about twelve Americans and eight Russians that we would meet once we got to Russia. This trip was being led by a man named Terry. His wife, Susan, and two young sons, Jonathan and Peter, would be going on this trip. This was to be the first of what was to become many trips to this orphanage. We wanted to establish a presence in Lyahi so the kids and staff would really get to know us. Terry had connections with a long-term American missionary in Russia named Jeanne Beckner who lived in Vladimir, Russia. Between the two of them, they would work out the plans for the two weeks we would spend in Russia. Terry had assembled a great team. We worked on music, drama, sports, games, Bible studies, and language for the kids. Excitement was building, and we could not wait to get to Lyahi. I took my keyboard to help with the music. As usual, we flew to New York's JFK airport and boarded a plane to Moscow. Flights to Russia are long, usually nine or ten hours from New York. Landing in Moscow, it was a mad dash to get through immigration. Lines were nonexistent in those days, and there was a lot of pushing to get up front. If several planes came in at the same time, it became a madhouse. After sitting on a plane for ten hours from New York, the confusion of the Moscow immigration area was pretty annoying, and you felt they must be able to do better than this. As soon as we arrived, we felt Satan at work even in the airport as the passport control officers detained one of our team members, Tim, for irregularities in his visa (the dates were incorrect). Our team immediately formed a circle in the airport and prayed that they would release Tim and let us proceed. This was Tim's first trip out of the United States, and understandably, he was shaken up, especially when they said they would put him on the first flight back to the US. This was our first crisis but certainly not our last as we saw God work in supernatural ways to get his work done each and every day. Prayer was our constant companion. The dates on Tim's visa were wrong, but they finally let him proceed, realizing that the error was probably made by the Russian Embassy in Washington.

After finally clearing customs, we left the airport for a one-night stay in the beautiful Moscow Marriott, which was a gift from the hotel's manager to our team. Our team leader Terry also worked for the Marriott chain in the US and knew the manager of the Moscow hotel. We were all very exhausted after traveling over twenty hours and looked forward to a good night's rest. The hotel staff were very gracious to our team, giving us a great dinner and, in the morning, breakfast. After breakfast in Moscow, we got back on the chartered bus for a three-hour trip to Vladimir. Now we will see the real Russia. Vladimir is a large city midway between Moscow and Lyahi. It has a population of about four hundred thousand and is over a thousand years old. There, we met up with our Russian translators. They were all great Christian brothers and sisters and spoke English very well. Most were in their late teens or early twenties. We also were introduced to the long-term Russian-based American missionary, Jeanne Beckner. We had been invited by the orphanage director to stay at a workers' camp adjoining the children's camp. There were about twenty of us, including the translators. On the ride to Lyahi, we sang, told jokes, and had a lot of fun on the bus. The entire time, I had memories of the orphanage in St. Petersburg and expected something similar in Lyahi. Boy, was I wrong.

As the bus entered the village of Lyahi, we were rather shocked at how run-down and poor it appeared. We were told that the village had about three thousand five hundred residents. The streets were filled with potholes, and most of the side streets were unpaved. Rather than the large communist era concrete block apartment buildings that seemed to dominate Moscow, St. Petersburg, and even Vladimir, Lyahi was mostly comprised of rather shabby single-family homes and a few communist-style concrete apartment buildings. The homes were small and generally constructed of wood. Most needed painting and repairs, and I found out later, many did not have running water or flush toilets. The village looked very old and worn.

Our team went directly to the camp known as Camp Ogonyock (Camp Fire in English) where there were cabins for the children. The team was supposed to stay at an adjacent camp a short distance from Camp Og (as it became known). However, when our bus arrived at the "workers' camp," we were met at the gate by a staff member who told us that we could not stay at the camp because we had not submitted health certificates to the state agency that oversees orphanages. This was allegedly to protect the orphans from diseases we might bring. We eventually found out the real reason was they did not want Christians to stay at the camp. We had to remember that Russia had been an officially atheistic society up until 1991, and many of the old attitudes and beliefs were still prevalent. At this point, we did not know what to do, as all our plans depended on the team staying at the camp at a very nominal cost. We were turned away from the camp and did not know where we would go. Someone in our group said, "Let's pray and see what the Lord will have us do." After prayer, the group sponsor, Jeanne, said that there was a small city called Murom about twenty miles from the camp. She suggested we should go there and see if they have a hotel that could accommodate us. Our group leader Terry said that he would have to ask each of us for funds to help pay for a hotel if there was one in Murom since hotel funds had not been in the team's budget.

We were all so disappointed but knew that the maxim we had been taught before we left was certainly needed now: "The flexible shall not be broken." We needed to be flexible, and it was just our second day in Russia. There were lots of jokes about the team sleeping on the bus. I noticed that our Russian translators did not seem particularly fazed by this turn of events. I realize that Russians are so used to disruptions, disappointments, and plans falling apart that it was just a normal day for them. They truly were flexible. Our driver took us to this city named Murom (with a population of one hundred sixteen thousand), which is one of the most ancient cities in Russia, part of the golden ring. It is over a thousand years old. It is home to the father of color photography, Sergey Prokudin-Gorsky, and the father of television, Vladimir Zworykin (1889). We found a low-priced hotel, the Hotel Lada. On the outside, it looked like it would be rated minus three stars. We found out that the City of Murom was a closed city until communism fell in the early nineties. A closed city in Russia is usually a city of great military importance. It is where military hardware, such as tanks, guns, grenades, explosives, etc., are manufactured. It also meant that prior to 1991, the residents could not leave the city, and people who didn't live in the city could not enter without special permission from the officials, which was difficult to get. We also found out that the residents of such closed cities were told to be extremely suspicious of foreigners, especially Americans, as Americans wanted to kill Russians and destroy the country with nuclear weapons. When the city started opening up in the early nineties, the attitudes of the people were ingrained with suspicion and hatred of foreigners, especially Americans. Most of the people of Murom had never traveled anywhere or met an American.

Hotel Lada was quite an experience. Checking into the hotel was very difficult. At first, they didn't want to allow our team to stay there. They said they didn't have enough rooms. Once we agreed to pay higher than the normal rate, they found rooms, and they agreed to let us stay. However, it took over three hours for all of us to get registered and into a room. In Russia, you have to surrender your passport to the hotel clerk who officially registers you as being in that city. There is a police requirement that one is only allowed to stay in a city for three days unless he or she reregisters with the police. Our rooms were up on the third floor, and of course, there were no elevators. We hauled our luggage upstairs and settled into our rooms. Each room had twin beds, and so two team members stayed in each room. There was a toilet and sink at the end of the hall and a single shower/tub on the other side of the hall. Immediately, we wondered how all of us would ever get showered and dressed in the morning with such limited facilities. Ultimately, it did work out. Some members showered in the evening, and some got up early in the morning to take a shower. The bedsheets were very thin, ragged, and worn; but it was all we had to sleep on. I think the hotel was quite embarrassed by the condition of the sheets because when we returned the next evening after camp, all the sheets had been replaced with brand-new ones. After an initial cold reception by the hotel staff, they warmed up and became very friendly even though we didn't understand what they were saying most of the time. We were warned by Jeanne and Terry never to venture outside alone as there was still intense hostility toward Americans in the city, and we would be objects of curiosity and possibly animosity. If we had to leave the hotel, we should always have someone accompany us.

One hot evening after a long day at the camp, I decided I wanted a soft drink. I knew the vendors at the kiosks on the street sold sodas, so I asked some of the guys if they would go out with me to get one. They all said they were wiped out and just wanted to rest. So I violated the rule and decided to go out on my own. How dangerous could this be? I walked out of the hotel and strolled down the street to a kiosk and bought a soda. As I walked back up the street to the hotel, a group of about ten young men cornered me and told me to sit down on a bench outside the hotel. I had no idea what was happening, but a little fear went through me as I remembered Jeanne's warnings. One of the young men, who was about eighteen, spoke English, although it was apparent none of the others did. He asked me who I was and why was I in Murom. I tried to explain our purpose for being there. He kept relaying everything I said to the others in Russian. After hearing me out, he finally said to me, "You have come all the way from Floreeda to help Russian children?" When he said that to the other guys, they looked at me as though I was a Martian or something. They had never heard of people doing such things. They had never heard of missionaries. I told him I felt we were doing God's work for the unfortunate orphans in Russia. I could sense they were really softening up and were very interested in what I had to say. I asked them if they would mind if I could get some of the other folks on our team to come out and meet them. They agreed, and I went into the hotel and told the others that they had to come outside and talk to these young men. Everyone jumped up; one guy grabbed his guitar, and they all made it hastily down the steps to the group outside. Our translators talked to the young men and explained salvation and God's plan for people. They listened intently. We started singing to them some of our Christian songs. It was a beautiful evening, and by the time it ended, I believe we had convinced them of God's love for them, and they said they would go to the Calvary Chapel in the Murom to learn more about our God.

Each morning, there was a bus call at nine o'clock. We were to be outside the hotel and ready to board the bus for the forty-minute trip to Camp Ogonyock. Once we got to the camp, we would have breakfast there before starting our planned activities. The camp was quite rustic with cabins that had sleeping facilities for about ten kids each and a main camp house. There were ninety kids in camp.

In the main camp house, there was a large day room and dining room along with a few rooms for staff sleeping. There were no bathrooms at the camp, just outhouses. The most difficult part of this trip was using outhouses, especially since they weren't clean. The kids, pretty much, cleaned themselves by swimming in the adjacent river. I don't know how it got there in the middle of the forest, but there was a beach along the river. The kids loved the beach and swimming in the river. The boys did not own swimming trunks, so they swam in their underwear. With a few exceptions, most of the girls did not go in the river because they didn't have bathing suits and were too embarrassed to go in their underwear.

There were no showers or bathing facilities in the main orphanage building either, although it did have running water. The orphanage children had to go into the village's public bathhouse (a *baña*) to take a "shower." The shower consisted of buckets of warm water that they poured over their heads, a soaping up, and then more buckets of water over their heads. The boys went one week and the girls the following week. The bottom line is that at most they could bathe once every two weeks. If a child misbehaved during the week, then even this bath would be taken away. Kids in orphanages do not enjoy being unclean any more than kids in nice middle-class homes. Personal toiletries were few and far between.

Contrary to popular opinion, Russia can get pretty hot in the middle of summer. The mosquitoes are huge. Normally, I am not bothered by mosquitoes at home, but these were different. They were two or three times the size of Florida mosquitoes. In the evenings, they attacked with a vengeance. I don't think they have heard of screens in Russia. I never saw any. Windows are just left open, and mosquitoes and flies can enter at will. We spent half the night killing bugs and insects before we could get to sleep, and then we had to keep the windows shut to keep out the mosquitoes and other flying insects. The rooms became like ovens.

The orphanage normally has about one hundred children during the school year, but some went to other camps or had gone to be with relatives for the summer. Although most did not speak a word of English, we seemed to have very little trouble communicating with hand signals, smiles, and lots of love. Our translators were invaluable. Most were young Christian men and women who loved working at the camp. We organized games, sports, taught songs, and had daily Bible studies. One of the highlights of each day was the time for arts and crafts. The kids were very talented and were able to paint very nice pictures and make all kinds of things with the craft materials we brought over. As the orphanage was very poor, we purchased additional food. We loaded the cooks up with vegetables, chicken, and beef to be cooked for the kids. They were getting wonderful balanced meals (with protein) for a change. Their regular diet consisted of some sort of hot cereal in the morning along with bread and milk. At lunchtime, they would get soup, bread, and tea. For dinner, they would again get soup, bread, and tea. Virtually, all the kids were skinny and looked undernourished. In spite of this, they did seem to be relatively healthy. There was a nurse assigned to the orphanage who oversaw their health needs, although she complained to us that she had virtually no supplies, especially antibiotics. Contrary to the initial description of the orphans, they did not seem to be learning disabled. Most were quite sharp and intelligent with a great sense of humor. Like our translators, they didn't seem to let too many things bother them.

Orphanages are known in Russia as "children's homes." The orphanage staff, although few in number, was excellent, especially the director, Valentina Milhaolvna. She had a very kind disposition and, from what we understood, was a great improvement from the former director who was harsh and cruel. Valentina was a well-educated woman, holding two university degrees. Previously, there had been cages in the orphanage to put children into when they misbehaved. Valentina had the cages removed and virtually eliminated corporal punishment. When kids misbehaved or violated the rules, they were assigned additional household chores such as scrubbing floors. One concern Valentina had was dearth of male staff. She had only one. With so many teen boys, she believed they needed more male influence. With a virtually all-female staff, she felt the boys' needs were being overlooked. She was very happy that our team was comprised of so many men who could take a direct interest in the boys. As it turned out, the male team members worked primarily with the boys, and the female team members worked with the girls. She said the reason the children's homes didn't attract men was because of the very low wages offered by the government.

Valentina allowed our team a lot of leeway in what we were planning to do. She did warn us that we should not attempt to convert any of the children, as it would offend the Russian Orthodox Church. We found out that the Russian Orthodox Church in Lyahi did not concern themselves with the orphanage. In fact, the children of the orphanage were considered second-class citizens and ignored even by the locals. The children who were considered academically normal went to the public school in town, and the kids who had emotional or academic problems were taught by teachers at the orphanage. The local kids often made fun of the orphanage kids because they did not have nice clothes. To get back at the town kids, the orphanage kids would sometimes strike out and beat one of them up. I asked Valentina if any of the adults in the town ever offered to volunteer at the orphanage, and she said "never." Even the priests of the church rarely paid a visit, and the children were never invited to church services.

Children could remain at the children's home until they turned sixteen and a half or graduated from high school, which in Russia is eleventh grade. If they hadn't managed to get to eleventh grade by their seventeenth birthday, they could stay at the orphanage until they were eighteen but no longer. When they left the orphanage, they were on their own. Many ended up moving to the cities, and if they weren't skilled enough to do some sort of manual work, some became prostitutes or got involved in the pornography industry. Most of the boys were taken into the army if they were physically healthy. As orphans, they were sent to serve in the worst and most remote parts of the country, usually Siberia. Boys from more affluent families could avoid such duty and served in very desirable areas of the country. It is difficult to get a decent job when you leave an orphanage. Generally, they have no marketable skills and had been prohibited by the government from attending college or university. At best, they could attend a government-run trade school. All the reports we heard were that the trade schools treated the students poorly. They lived in dangerous dorms where assaults and rapes were common. Most of the kids left the trade schools before they completed the training out of fear for their safety. Without at least some training, they were doomed to be at the bottom of Russian society, economically and culturally. It is no wonder the Russian prisons have a high proportion of orphans in them. Many resort to stealing and breaking into houses to find a place off the streets. As everyone knows, Russia is brutally cold in the winter, and there is no way one could survive in a box or a tent in the park. I had been to Russia several times in midwinter and can attest to the frigid conditions. Once when I was there with a winter team, the temperature fell to forty degrees below zero in Lyahi. I think the warmest the orphanage got up to during that time was about fifty-to-fifty-five degrees because one of the furnaces was broken and not providing heat. The whole time I was there, I slept in my clothes. To make matters worse, I came down with a bad cold and had no medication to help me. After a day or so, one of the boys, Lev, came over to me with some black liquid that he told me to drink. I drank it, and amazingly, I started feeling better. To this day, I still don't know what that disgusting-tasting liquid was, but it sure did work.

I would eventually go on four team trips to Lyahi, two in summer and two in winter. The summer trips were camps, and the winter trips were to help the kids celebrate the holidays—Christmas and New Year. In Russia, New Year is a bigger celebration than Christmas. It is probably the biggest holiday of the year. Christmas is more low-key and celebrated primarily by Christians.

The dynamics of living in a children's home are very peculiar to outsiders. It appears that, due to a lack of sufficient staff, the older children are able to dominate the younger children. The older boys, who are decidedly taller and stronger than the little kids, can be bullies at times. But in all the weeks I spent at the home, I never observed a boy trying to intimidate a girl. For the most part, the home was pretty peaceful. I felt that the staff that were there, even though few in number, did an excellent job considering the circumstances. The discipline we observed was not corporal punishment but included such things as having the children scrub floors or do extra kitchen duty. It was somewhat easy to observe that the older boys dominate the younger boys (and girls) through intimidation. We understand that fighting was not tolerated and would bring swift punishment for the offenders. Our team did not observe any fighting among the children during our visit, but we know from talking to younger children that they did have some fear of the older boys who would steal from them. We also found out that some of the older boys did occasionally obtain cigarettes and alcohol and would become intoxicated. The alcohol they consumed was mostly home-brewed stuff from the village. People make a form of vodka at home because it is cheaper than buying it at a kiosk or store.

Life in the orphanage was difficult at best. One of the things I did not understand was how the food was apportioned. It didn't seem to matter the age or size of the child; everyone got exactly the same amount of food. Sixteen-year-old boys and girls certainly eat more than an eight-year-old child, but everyone got the same amount. I could see why the older boys and girls were so skinny. There was no going back for seconds most of the time because the cooks only prepared enough food for the number of children they were going to feed. I did notice that most of the cooks were quite chunky though. The cooks fed the staff workers and visitors prior to giving the children their food. I understand that some of the children volunteered to work in the kitchen because they would get extra food from the cooks.

According to the director, Valentina, one of the biggest problems she faced was the lack of funding from the government. She was receiving about three dollars per month for each child, and this was for food, clothing, and medical care. At times, she and the staff did not receive their salaries for months on end. She felt very thankful, and amazed, that her staff did not leave her and the children. There were times when there was absolutely no food to feed the children, and the kids had to go roaming through the local farms to find potatoes or other items to keep from starving. Some of the boys had been arrested for stealing potatoes from local farmers. And the home itself was in need of major repairs, along with painting. Many of the beds and mattresses were coming apart. Electric wires were not concealed in conduits and looked quite dangerous.

At times our team felt very helpless, wanting to really change things but not being able to. Our hearts bled for the children and the staff. Interestingly, the children did not appear to be unhappy in their circumstances, possibly because they were used to the circumstances and didn't know anything different. Generally, the children were pretty upbeat, and they were always ready to play a game or to engage in activities the team planned. It was only when you engaged a child one on one that they would express some sadness at not being with their families or not having a family. This was especially true when we visited during the Christmas/New Year holidays when some children who had families went to be with them. Sometimes an aunt or cousin came to get them for a few days, but rarely a parent. Looking at these dear children who had no one who cared about them was heartbreaking. It was difficult to imagine how someone could care so little about a child that they brought into the world and could just leave them in such a place. Valentina, the director, told me that in all the time she had been there, not one parent had ever redeemed his or her child, and they had had only one adoption by an outside family (an American family). It should be noted that the director did ask our team if any of us were interested in adopting a child. We felt that it wasn't the reason we were there, and so we all declined. Not out of lack of interest but because we knew that if we got involved in adoptions, our mission would be compromised by possibly showing favoritism to a child that was selected for adoption. The truth is most of us, if we could have afforded it, would have adopted all the children. None of the team members had ever been to an orphanage before our trips to Russia. We had no idea what they were like or how the children would be. We didn't know that the children would tug at our heartstrings. We didn't know that we could love dozens of children that we had never met before. After our two-week camps, leaving the orphanage on the last day was painful. Usually, everyone was in tears, the team as well as the children, who kept asking us to return. The bus ride from the camp back to the airport was very solemn with everyone sharing their desire to return.

During this first summer encampment in 2000, I spent most of my time with the boys. We were engaged in the morning in sporting activities and swimming. In the afternoons, we had worship and Bible study. The older boys (ages twelve and up) were involved in the "Boys' Club." The Boys' Club was held each afternoon outside the main building. The boys were set in a circle, and we taught the life of

Joseph from the Book of Genesis. The point was to show these boys that even though Joseph was sold off into slavery by his brothers and he spent years in prison for something he didn't do, God was able to give him a life that is still talked about thousands of years later. We wanted the life of Joseph to be an inspiration to these boys who now had no one to depend on but God. Because most did not have good earthly fathers, we emphasized how God was our heavenly father and cared for us more than any earthly father ever could. Even though some of the oldest boys initially expressed hostility to the idea of joining in the Bible study, after a few days, they all joined in and looked forward to the Boys' Club each afternoon. I was taken aback one session when I asked one of the boys, Kolya, if he would like one day to be second in command in Russia just as Joseph became second in command in Egypt. He gave me a very strange look as though that was the most ridiculous question he had ever heard. In his mind, that would be absolutely impossible. He answered, "No." I asked him what he would like to become. He said he would become whatever "they" made him become. I died a little inside realizing that choice is a very "American" idea. In Russia, you become what "they" decide you will become especially if you are an orphan or poor. The interesting thing about Kolya is that he was one of the very few children who spoke English. He had been adopted previously by a Russian Christian family. They sent him to a private Christian school where he learned English. He was with the family for five years. They had adopted five children from various orphanages and had four of their own. For whatever reason, the mom and dad divorced and placed all nine of their children in orphanages. This was Kolya's second stint in an orphanage. Kolya was always willing to help the team in whatever we needed and was able to help us with language problems. He also was thrilled at the opportunity to practice his English. He was one of the older boys, at about fourteen. It was the first time that I thought about the possibility of trying to help a child get adopted.

Another boy who showed great interest in our team and in me was a boy of twelve named Lev. He called me "Fred Fred." Why he said my name twice, I don't know, but I found it quite endearing. Many of the kids tried to learn some English words as we tried to learn Russian words. Amazingly, we were always able to communicate in some way even when the translators weren't available at the moment. Lack of language knowledge did not stop us. When we were playing sports, Lev always seemed to want to be on my team. We developed quite a friendship in those two weeks. On the last day, we planned a party for the kids and invited the worship band from Calvary Chapel in Murom to come and play. (They came and played, and we had plenty of food as the kids danced and enjoyed themselves.) I don't know how they did it, but the kids all came to the party spruced up. The girls had done their hair and had on nice dresses, and the boys were very duded up with their hair slicked back and nice clean clothes on. They were truly ready for a party. Near the end of the time for the party, one of the brothers, Tolli, from Calvary Chapel Murom, decided to give a message of salvation to the children. He eloquently explained the Gospel, and at the end, he gave an invitation for the children to accept Jesus as their Lord and Savior. I was somewhat nervous as the director and the teachers were all in the room, and we had been told expressly not to give a salvation invitation as it would bring problems from the Russian Orthodox priests in the town. However, once Tolli got started, he couldn't stop, and he asked the children who wanted to give their lives to the Lord to stand up. Over half the children stood up. The director, Valentina, never said a word at the time or later. I (and I believe all our team) wanted to cry tears of joy at what happened. This had to be a work of the Lord. Brother Tolli was like an angel sent from heaven. He did what none of us would have done since we agreed that we wouldn't. However, Tolli wasn't there for the agreement, and he didn't know that he could not give an invitation to the children. We weren't there, but the following day, Tolli came back and baptized in the river those kids who had accepted the Lord, and Lev was one of them.

On that last night, the team had filled up one thousand water balloons to have a fight, team and staff against the children. Before we got on the bus, we commenced the fight. Balloons were flying through the air, and the team was soaked. The kids really beat us good as they were faster at getting additional balloons and were deadly accurate in their aim. We laughed and cried as we hugged the children before getting on the bus. The bus was surrounded by kids waving and crying. As the bus was slowly moving out down the wooded lane, I saw Lev standing beside my window with tears flowing down his cheeks as he waved good-bye. It is simply amazing how attached we had become after spending only two weeks with the children. All our hearts were touched by our experience.

For folks who have been on mission trips especially to orphanages, they know the difficulty in leaving never knowing what will happen to the children or if they will ever see them again. During the two weeks we were with the children, we grew close to all of them and truly bonded with some. Many times I heard team members say how they wish they could adopt all the kids and bring them to the US. (What gave us peace was the knowledge that we had imparted as much knowledge as we could to them about the Lord Jesus Christ and that we were able to be with them in a warm and intimate way.) The children loved the attention, and in many ways, we were fascinating to them, as we came from a land far away showering them with love. This is not to say that the staff did not try to fulfill their needs, but the staff was limited in what they could do. Virtually, all the staff were women who had difficulty understanding the needs of the boys, especially the teenage boys. Plus, they were in the position of having to discipline the children, probably more than they were able to show affection. It appeared that the staff went out of their way to keep from showing favoritism to any one child.

Our team, which included Russians and Americans, was absolutely awesome in the way everyone worked together to give the children a wonderful summer camp experience. The Russians, most of whom were young adults, spoke very good English even though they had never been out of Russia. They said they learned English by watching English-language TV and going to movies that were in English. For Americans, the Russian language is quite difficult as it uses the Cyrillic alphabet, which is totally different than the Latin alphabet we use in America. Even the Russians felt English was easier to learn than Russian. It has thirty-two letters that are difficult to even pronounce. We did our best to learn Russian phrases, and it was a great help even if it brought laughter from the kids at times.

On the bus returning to the hotel in Murom, most of us were in quiet reflection. Realizing in two days we would be returning home was somewhat sad. I know I could have easily spent another two weeks at the camp. That evening, we were very busy packing and making sure we had all the documents needed to exit Russia the next day without any problems. The next morning, we had a six-hour bus ride back to Moscow. We were welcomed back at the Grand Marriott Hotel in Moscow, where the manager had promised us we could spend our last night without charge. What a change from our time in Lyahi and Murom. We were treated to a great dinner, and the next morning, we had a wonderful breakfast before going to the airport for our one o'clock noon flight back to New York and Tampa.

Our Delta flight to New York was long and tedious. The airline had all of us in a group. I was sitting just behind two folks from our trip, a guy and a gal, and I could hear their conversation. The guy had been a very big nuisance to the team. He was the least cooperative and had gotten so out of hand by his behavior that midway during the trip, the team leader had called Calvary Chapel in St. Petersburg, Florida, to see what to do with him. The kids at the camp had reported him as being overly aggressive and rough toward them during sports activities. As much as the staff enjoyed our team, they were not happy with this fellow (whom, for this story, I will call Jim). The pastor suggested sending him home. However, when approached by the team leader, he promised to follow the rules and that we would have no more trouble with him. One thing that bothered me and others was that Jim spent an inordinate amount of time taking digital photos of the kids. It must have been hundreds, if not thousands. He had been told not to bring his laptop computer on the trip, which he did anyhow. Laptop computers in 2000 were very expensive, and we had no place to store such equipment. Unfortunately, he was my roommate in Murom and Moscow. He was so disturbing to me that I asked Terry to reassign me to another room, or I would sleep in the hallway if necessary. Every morning at about two or three o'clock, Jim would get up, turn on his computer, and begin looking at all the pictures he had taken, making as much noise as possible. Terry reassigned me to a room with one of the Russian team members, Dima, which gave me great peace.

On the plane, I listened to Jim, who had a very unusual interest in one of the teen girls, Luba, at the camp and spent a lot of time talking to her. He told his seatmate that he was planning to come back to Russia to try and adopt Luba. I couldn't believe my ears. I did not want to believe the Russian officials would let this man adopt a young girl. As his conversation continued, I heard him say that if he couldn't adopt Luba, he would adopt Lev. I was so upset by his statements that I could not enjoy my flight. In the meantime, Jim saw a young girl walking around the cabin of the jet and called her over to his seat. The girl was about five or six years old. Jim started talking to her, picking her up and putting her on his lap, and tickling her. Then he started lifting her into the air in what appeared to me to be his attempt to look under her dress. Our team leader's wife, who was sitting across from him and observing Jim, screamed at him to put the girl down and to send her back to her parents who were sitting on the other side of the wide body jet and couldn't see what Jim was doing. I was so disgusted by his behavior that I had a hard time speaking civilly to him. By this time, his seatmate was in tears. I kept thinking that I don't know how I will do it, but I'll never let Jim adopt Luba or my little friend Lev. They deserved better than that. I started drafting the letter I would write to the orphanage hopefully to prevent Jim from adopting any of the children.

We finally landed in New York, and after being processed through immigration and customs, we caught our flight to Tampa. I was dead tired when I got home; however, I couldn't get Jim's statements out of my mind, and I was determined to save those kids from him.

CHAPTER 4

Let's Get Lev Out

The trip to the orphanage in Lyahi had been one of the highlights of my life. By far, it was the most satisfying mission trip I had been on. However, I was still hounded by Jim's statements about adopting the teen girl Luba or Lev. Since I had spent most of my time working with the boys, I didn't know Luba as well. However, I had heard that she was a somewhat troubled girl and had run away several times and had been found with young men. I think that is what attracted Jim to her. She had no living parents or relatives who wanted her, so the orphanage might be happy to be rid of her. On the other hand, Lev was a nice young boy who really seemed to enjoy the mission team. He participated in all the activities. Since I knew him quite well, I decided to see if I could find someone who might be interested in adopting him and getting him out of the orphanage. I started talking to friends and others to see if anyone would have the heart to adopt a nice Russian boy. The response I kept getting was that since I knew him, why didn't I adopt him? That was not something I had even considered. First of all, I was just getting out of a marriage and didn't feel that adoption was something I should or could do without a wife. However, no matter how many people I approached, they kept saying the same thing. "Why don't you adopt him?" The more I thought about the idea of adopting this boy, the more it seemed to make some sense. However, I did not have any idea if he was adoptable or if I would even qualify to adopt. Most amazingly, I never once considered that this boy might be the answer to my prayer in 1997 to have another son. I guess I never thought God would answer my prayer in this way. I had thought of all kinds of ways for God to answer my request, but never in a thousand years would I have imagined this scenario. All the way to Russia to find what God had for me? Is this real or is my imagination running away with me again? I had thought up many ways for God to answer my prayer. The most real for me was to marry a woman who had a son without a dad and adopt him. However, every woman I met who fit that description disappeared before we even had a chance to date.

I decided that before I did anything, I should write to the orphanage director Valentina and find out if Lev was available for adoption and also ask if she thought I was qualified to adopt him. She wrote me back and said that he was available for adoption, and I would qualify to adopt him. This raised my spirits a bit. A couple of weeks later, I received the following letter from Lev. It was written in Russian and given to one of the Russian team members, Pasha, to send to me. Pasha translated the letter and sent it to me. Here is what it said:

August 20, 2000

Hi, Fred!
  This is your brother Lev from Lyahi camp. You should remember me because we were there in the camp together. How is your health? How is life in general? Do you miss me? Because I really miss you. I'm doing good; health is good

as well. Thank you for the alarm clock that you left with me, but somebody has stolen it from me. But actually, we were able to find them, and the teachers keep it for me now. We are good friends with Pasha, and we are practicing some karate with him. If you have a chance to send me a little book with karate pictures, please do because I want to learn it.

Please keep me in your prayers so I could grow in the Lord and please send me your picture so I can pray for you.

Good-bye. I'll wait for your letter.

With respect,
Lev

I was so surprised to get the letter but very happy. I sent one back to him.

September 9, 2000

Dear Lev,

How are you, my brother? I hope this letter finds you happy. It has taken me a long time to write to you because I didn't have your mailing address. Everything is fine with me. I am in good health and am happy. I think about you all the time and look forward to the time when I will see you again. I am very happy that the brothers from Calvary Chapel Vladimir were able to install showers for the children. What a blessing. I sent you a package containing some clothes, pictures, and a karate book. I sure hope you receive them. I sent them on September 6, 2000, and the post office told me it would take approximately ten days for you to receive it. I have a few rubles left and will send them so hopefully you can purchase stamps.

How are your Bible studies going? Are the brothers from Calvary Chapel Murom still coming by the children's home?

I pray for you and especially that Jesus will be with you every day giving you happiness and peace. I am planning a trip back to Lyahi for a Christmas camp and hope to spend a lot of time with you then. I am trying to learn to speak more Russian so we can talk when I get there. I have been praying to God as to how he can make me a part of your life. Please pray for me that I will be obedient to the Lord and do his will.

Lev, let me know if you have any special needs that I can help you with. You can talk to me about anything at anytime. Continue to be an example to the others who don't know Christ.

Your brother and friend,
Fred

I was now even more encouraged to pursue the adoption. Old thoughts surfaced about my being a black American trying to adopt a green-eyed, blond-haired Russian boy. Would the officials ever approve such an arrangement? In the US, that might be quite difficult although not particularly difficult for a Caucasian to adopt an African American child. However, this was Russia, not the US. Before I would officially start the process or worry too much about the racial issue, I needed to know if Lev wanted to be adopted by me. I sent Pasha an e-mail and asked that he go to the orphanage and talk to Lev to see if he wanted to be adopted by me. I also let Jeanne Beckner know that I was interested in adopting Lev. A week or two later, Pasha sent me an e-mail and told me that Lev did want to be adopted by me. This is what I needed to hear.

On September 12, 2000, I received the following e-mail from Jeanne:

> Dear Fred:
>
> Lev's name is Lev Migalinski, not a typical Russian name, sounds more Polish or Jewish. His birth date is June 3, 1987. One of the requirements of the new adoption laws is that the parent must travel to Russia twice—once to identify the child and the second for the court. You have already met that first requirement. Be sure and save your plane stubs/itinerary from the camp trip. I would suggest at this point, you begin your home study ASAP. This is the most time-consuming. Any licensed social worker can do this, and she will know all the information needed. Also, your letter of intention to adopt Lev needs to be faxed to the adoption center here in Vladimir ASAP. This puts Lev on the registry for international adoption. He must be there for six months before he can leave Russia. It will be the best if Lev can be adopted before his fourteenth birthday. Pasha and I were pray-

ing for you and this wonderful blessing for Lev
this morning.

International adoptions are not easy, and adoptions from Russia
are quite difficult unless you meet every criterion to a T. Additionally,
Russia had been threatening during that time to eliminate American
adoptions altogether (which they finally did a few years later). In
September 2000, I sent an official application to the director of the
The Center of Adoption, Custody and Guardianship for the Vladimir
region that Lev was in. It had all the information that Russia requires
(I thought). I received a terse letter back from the director, Nadezhda
Nikolayevna. She basically told me that Lev was not available for
adoption because his father was still living and had not relinquished
custody of him. Also, she said that I did not qualify to adopt because
I was past the preferred age of adoptive parents (fifty) and I was not
married. In Russia at that time, unmarried people, unlike in the
United States, were not permitted to adopt. They also preferred couples under age fifty. She said she would not consider my application.
I was crushed by this news. I think what bothered me most was the
fact that they didn't seem to consider the fact that I could offer him
a good home and that he would have opportunities in the US that
he as an orphan would never be able to find in Russia as orphans are
at the bottom of the social scale in Russia. They are referred to as the
"forgotten children." Additionally, most adopting families, American
or otherwise, want babies or toddlers, not teenagers. Russian citizens
do not normally adopt children who are not close relatives, so the
orphanages are burgeoning with children who will never be adopted
by anyone. I was an anomaly: someone wanting to adopt a child who
was almost a teenager. Russian orphanages were bursting at the seam
with almost a million orphans.

Lev had been in the orphanage for about five years at this point.
The reason he was there was that his mother had passed away when

he was four years old. He then went to live with his grandmother in Vladimir. He lived with her for four years, and then she had a stroke. The stroke paralyzed her, and she was unable to care for an eight-year-old boy. The state removed him from her care and placed him in a children's home. His father had abandoned the family just before his mom died. At this point, Lev was alone, although he expressed to me how much love he had for his grandmother. They used to go by train to their dacha (a small plot of farmland given by the government for growing crops), and he and his grandmother would plant potatoes and other crops that would help them get through the awful Russian winters.

I did not know what to do at this point. Now that Lev knew that I wanted to adopt him, what would I now tell him? I decided that I couldn't let Nadezhda's letter be the final authority. I started thinking about the racial factor again, wondering if that was the reason for the denial. I had no evidence that it was an issue; it just sat in the back of my mind. I sat down and wrote her a three-page letter detailing why I thought the policy made no sense and that Lev's future, if he stayed at the orphanage, would doom him to a life of poverty and hopelessness. I also told her what she already knew: that most Russian male orphans end up in jail or the army. The girls do not fare much better, with many ending up in large cities as prostitutes or menial workers in factories. I sent the letter to her hoping it might help. I explained to her what I thought I would be able to offer Lev. All kids in orphanages would like nothing better than to be a part of a family, whether biological or adopted. I received a letter back from her several weeks later. She informed me that the rules were the rules. I did not qualify, and my application would not be considered. I felt my hopes were dashed, and so I prayed and asked the Lord for guidance. Should I accept the rejection or should I continue to try and change her mind?

I sent a letter to my missionary friend Jeanne in Russia. I asked her if she would prevail upon Nadezhda since she knew her from previous attempts at adoption by an American family. Jeanne wrote me back and said that she had gone to the Nadezhda's office to ask her to consider my application. She said that Nadezhda was very adamant that she would not change her mind and would refuse any more petitions from me. She told Jeanne that there was no way that I would be able to adopt Lev. She reminded Jeanne that his biological father was alive as well and that I did not conform to the rules that required adoptive parents to be married and under age fifty. Children who have biological parents cannot be adopted unless the court takes away their parental rights and frees them up for adoption—first, by a relative, then by Russian couples. If no one comes forward, an international adoption will be considered. The news was depressing. I did not know what to do at this point. Should I continue or should I just let it go? Again, I prayed and asked God for a sign. Please, God, what is your will?

It was a Sunday morning in the fall of 2000. I went to church and picked up a copy of *The Heartbeat*, a church newsletter. There was a front-page article about a missionary couple from Calvary Chapel serving long term in Bolivia. This was a retired couple, Paul and Dori Pittman, who never had children of their own. The story related how a young sixteen-year-old Quechua Indian girl gave birth to a baby and promptly rejected him, refusing to nurse or care for him. The father expressed his rejection by disappearing. The Quechua people were suffering greatly from harsh economic conditions. Bolivian law had been recently changed in an effort to make it easier for both Bolivians and foreign residents to adopt. The Pittmans prayed and felt an assurance from God that they should adopt this little Quechan boy. It was a tremendous struggle to get the parents to go to court and to complete all the paperwork and home study, but finally the Pittmans were granted custody of the child with the adoption pending. The judge did say that they should try to find another child so that this young boy wouldn't grow up alone. They did that by finding a little baby girl that had been abandoned on a garbage dump. They were eventually able to finalize the adoption of both children. When I read this story, I felt that it was a sign from God that I should continue my quest to adopt Lev. If this retired couple who had never been blessed with a child could have that desire fulfilled so late in life, I now know that nothing was impossible with God. This article appeared just when I truly needed it as I was thinking about giving up.

I was in a quandary. What do I do to convince the authorities in Russia that I would be a good dad and to let Lev go? First of all, I must complete all the paperwork necessary. I contacted an adoption agency called Gift of Life who said they specialized in international adoptions. They agreed to take my case for a fee of one thousand five hundred dollars plus expenses. They would perform a home study and do the necessary paperwork to facilitate the adoption. (They did a home study, and I was approved, but when I asked about the necessary paperwork for the Russian officials, they admitted that they had lost their license to work in Russia.) Wow. Another problem I didn't foresee. I started searching for another adoption agency that could complete the paperwork. Jeanne gave me the name of an agency outside of Chicago called Uniting Families that was quite successful in processing adoptions in the Vladimir region of Russia. I contacted them and told them of my desire to adopt Lev. They said that they could do it and would send me paperwork to fill out and return with a five-hundred-dollar deposit. (I sent in the papers and the deposit, but a few days later, I received a phone call from Uniting Families saying they would have to decline to assist in this adoption because they noticed that I was divorced, which they said would make it impossible for me to adopt in that region.) I literally begged them to go forward with the case, but they insisted that single people cannot adopt in Russia. They didn't understand the law, but they had been working in Russia for years and did not want to take my money knowing I would be unsuccessful. I said that I would take full responsibility for the outcome, and I was aware of the risks. I begged them to do the paperwork even though they were sure I would be unsuccessful. Finally, the president of the agency, Mrs. Lynn Wetterburg, told me that they would reluctantly go ahead and do the application but wouldn't take any money from me unless I was successful, which they highly doubted I would be.

I never knew how much paperwork was involved in an international adoption. Not only must a detailed application be completed with photos but I had to get letters of recommendation from at least five people who knew me intimately. I needed to submit an application to the US Department of Justice, Immigration and Naturalization Service for permission to bring a foreign national into the US. I needed to submit copies of my tax returns, get a complete physical examination, have the FBI do a background fingerprint check, and submit dozens of other documents including photos of each room of my home. I had to successfully complete a training program for preadoptive families adopting institutionalized children. This was especially important for persons adopting from foreign orphanages, as virtually every child in such a situation has emotional problems related to being institutionalized. Each document had to be notarized with an Apostille stamp, each of which cost ten dollars and must be obtained from the Florida Department of State in Tallahassee. Hundreds of dollars later, spent on notaries and Apostille stamps, I had completed my dossier. The dossier was a big three-ring binder, three inches thick, filled with information, and it was required to be tied with a pretty ribbon and bow. Why a ribbon and bow? I have no idea. Once the dossier was completed, it had to be sent to Nadezhda at the Office of Custody, Guardianship, and Adoptions in Vladimir, Russia. Since Jeanne lived in Vladimir, I planned to send it to Jeanne and asked her to deliver it personally to the office. Jeanne felt it would be better if I brought it with me when

I came and presented it in person. She warned me about Nadezhda's hostility toward this adoption and to be prepared to be mistreated by her. I told Jeanne I would like to have her give it to Nadezhda since she has dealt with her in the past. I told her I would send the dossier to her by another couple traveling to Vladimir.

On November 2, 2000, I received the following letter from one of the camp translators and my friend, Dmitry Nikitin:

Hi, dear Fred!

This is Dmitry.

Thanks a lot for the gifts that you have sent to me and Paul. I and he were very excited. Everything fits very well. I was shocked when I saw this big box at the post office. It cost a lot to get it over here. Well, like here, that money is a lot. So thank God and to you. That was a big surprise.

We (me with the drama group and Pasha B) went to Lyahi a couple of weeks ago. It was great to see everyone there. I missed every kid there. So we went there to show some dramas that we had prepared and some gifts for the staff and other people. Afterward, we had much time to spend with the kids. Pasha B spend some time with Lev. He is fine, and he got everything you sent him. He seems to be fine emotionally except for one thing. I don't know if Pasha told you yet or not, but when we spoke with Lev, he seemed to be a little sad, so I asked him what was wrong, and he answered that his grandmother has recently died. He wasn't big-time bummed out, just a little sad.

I am sure that Pasha wrote you about his conversation with Lev, and I don't know all the details, but Lev now knows about your dossier to adopt him, and he is very excited. Oh, not only excited but I know all his life will change. Praise God! I hope everything will go smoothly and fine. May God direct... may God bless you, my brother.

Your friend,
Dmitry, Agape

In the meantime, Lev and I were exchanging letters frequently. He would write the letters in Russian and give them to Pasha who would translate them into English and forward them to me. I would send my letters to Pasha, who would translate them into Russian and take them to the orphanage and give them to Lev.

On December 14, 2000, I received a letter from the Office of Custody, Adoptions, and Guardianship. It was in Russian, so I asked my friend Cezar if he could try and translate it since he understands Polish, and there are similarities. This what the letter says:

In response to your adoption letter sent to the department of families in the Vladimirsky region, we inform you that Lev Olegorich Migalinski—born June 3, 1987, located in children's home of the Melekovsky region—is not adoptable at the present and not until the boy's father relinquishes his parental rights. Children's home has already submitted related paperwork to the appropriate court to initiate that process. If the boy's father relinquishes his parental rights, you will be able to adopt him no sooner than August 2001.

Additionally, usually during adoption proceedings, priority is given to full families. In your letter, nothing is mentioned about your marital situation… In connection with that, we ask you—[And here are two words that I do not understand. I have to look them up in the dictionary tonight.] I think they ask you to fulfill this missing information…

This was indeed good news. Now, it seemed as though things were starting to progress, and maybe our trials would be over. On December 8, 2000, Lev wrote the following letter:

Hello dear and much respected by me, Fred:

I got a free moment and wanted to write you a letter which I do. I think about you every day. And I want to see you. We just had our first school break. I did pretty good in this first semester but not as I wanted to be. German language is very hard for me. I'll put more effort in the second semester.

Winter starts here. We got the first snow and have frosts here and there. In the orphanage where we live, it's very warm though because we have gasificated heat. But the school is total opposite, very, very cold. We get so cold there, so at least they feed us good, and we can handle it. Our clothes are good too. So generally we are doing good, but I still think about you a lot and wait for your coming.

While in the vacation, I didn't go anywhere but stayed here in the orphanage. Fred, on October 1, my grandma died. She was the only one of my relatives that I had. I lived through the loss heavily. So now I don't have anywhere to go, and nobody needs me but you.

I read the Bible and learn to do good things.

Fred, please write me some more about your life there in Florida. About your home and life and pets and the things you do. Are your parents alive? Just your life. And with this, I will say good-bye. I love you very much and so appreciate our friendship.

I'll wait for your letter.

In Jesus,
Lev

CHAPTER 5

First Winter
Holiday Camp
December/January 2000

The church had announced a two-week winter camp for December 2000 at the orphanage, and of course, I was excited to sign up. During this camp, we were given permission to stay right in the orphanage. We were going to set up a holiday (Christmas/New Year) camp for the kids. One thing I forgot about Russia was how cold it gets in the winter. It was extremely cold, especially coming from Florida, but most of our activities were indoors. The kids cut down a tree in the woods to set up a Christmas tree in the day room. They made all the decorations by hand, and when they were finished, it looked great. We taught them Christmas songs and told them the story of Jesus's birth. We even made a bonfire in front of the building and had the kids roast marshmallows (something they had never done before). All in all, our time together was awesome, and the team became very close. Most of our Russian team members had been on the summer camp trip, and so it was like being with old friends. The children seemed to love that we had returned from the summer camp. Lev was very happy to see me, especially since he knew that I was planning to adopt him. The orphanage staff treated us like family as we were the first team to make a winter trip there. Because we were aware that the orphanage did not have enough funds to give the kids gifts for Christmas, we brought gifts for each child. We also purchased lots of food so that the kids' stomachs would be full over this holiday time. Bathing was a problem because only ice-cold water came from the sinks, and there were no flush toilets in the lavatories. There were no showers at this time, so all bathing was done standing next to a sink. One evening, one of our American team members, Derek, decided he really wanted to wash his hair, so he filled a sink with ice-cold water and stuck his head in it. Afterward, he had a "brain freeze" for an hour. We had warned him not to do that, but he did it anyhow and provided us with a lot of laughs afterward. All those little luxuries we were used to at home simply did not exist here, but you can survive it if you keep your sense of humor. We truly got to see what the kids dealt with all the time. During our evenings, we sang songs using the guitars that Dima and others had with them.

During our holiday camp, Lev and I really bonded, and he started calling me "Daddy." He was so eager to be adopted and to leave the orphanage. The other kids would tease him about that.

On our last day at the orphanage, we had a bang-up party for the children and staff. Before we left, we talked to Valentina about the team coming back for another summer camp in 2001. She thought it was a great idea and invited us to stay at the camp but to bring health certificates to satisfy the authorities. All we had to do was get permission from our church for another trip. As usual, we were all in tears as we left to go to Vladimir for an overnight stay before going on to Moscow for our flight home.

Coming home, I was hoping there would be some more news from Russia about the adoption. There was nothing. Lev and I continued writing to each other, and he was excited that the team would be coming back in summer. I do believe he was hoping the process would speed up, and so was I. It was my intention when I returned during this trip to Russia to visit his grandmother to reassure her that Lev would be okay and I had every intention of being a good dad to him. However, before I could go back, she had passed away. I received a letter from Lev telling me that his grand mom had died and that by the time the orphanage got him back to Vladimir, the funeral had already occurred, and his grandmother had been buried next to his mom. He was totally heartbroken as he felt he never had a chance to say good-bye to her. My heart was broken as I realized that grandmom was his last real link with his preorphanage childhood and anyone in Russia who truly loved him.

On January 29, 2001, I received the following letter from Lev:

Hello, my dear daddy,

This is your son Lev writing to you. You know I miss you very much and sometimes even cry for you. I very much want to see you, Dad. Other than that, I'm doing okay. Remember you gave me twenty dollars, and Pasha had it. Well, I still can't decide what to buy with it. I think I will buy a photo camera. I think that will be very good for me. Please write to me how you are doing and how's your health. Not too long ago, I got this package from an aunt (or just a lady), and there was a lot of everything in it. Also, please say thank you to that lady that gave money to me. Dad, please say hello to everybody from me. I'm sorry that my letter is so short. I don't know what else to say.

Good-bye, my best daddy in the world. I will wait for your letter back.

Children going swimming in the river at Camp Og during summer 2001

Boys doing crafts during summer camp

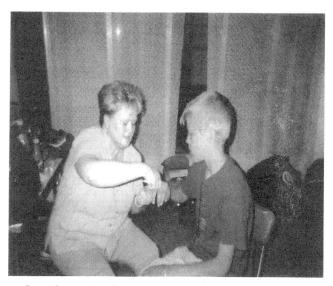

Lev getting a manicure from team member during summer, 2000

Lev and Fred outside Children's Home, winter, 2000

Mission Team outside Children's Home during Christmas Camp, Dec. 2001

Children singing Christmas songs during winter camp, Dec. 2001

Lev and Fred at camp Lyahi, Russia 2001

Photo taken during Christmas Camp, December 2001

74

Lev singing during winter camp, Dec. 2001

Foot washing ceremony and the presentation of new shoes
to all of the children

A letter from Jeanne arrived on February 4, 2001.

Dear Fred,

We went to Lyahi on Thursday. It was another special time with the children. Alya taught the lessons in the house on the valley where we lived. It just amazes me to see how they brighten up during this time. They were attentive and interested. We also added a conversational English lesson, and learning the English was really exciting to them, and they all had a great time. I spoke to Valentina about your situation. At the present moment, the only judge for the court in Melinki is on vacation. She will return in the next week, and they are asking her to hear Lev's case as soon as she opens her court (to remove his father's parental rights). I will see Tonya this weekend and understand clearly what your situation is. I do understand from the adoption center that they have notified the court to also complete Lev's case.

There was a conflict between Pasha and I concerning the gun he purchased for Lev. I didn't know you had given Pasha permission to buy this for Lev. He bought it, and I just happened to notice it in a bag he brought and left here at my flat. My objections are strong, and I share them with you. I have prayed and asked the Lord for wisdom and guidance. In Russia, there is not private ownership of handguns. They are an illegal item. Only gangsters and criminals have them. There is no "right to bear arms" amendment in this country. The gun is plastic but very realistic in appearance, and it shoots plastic pellets. People in America, even young boys, have been shot by police after pulling a gun like this on them. I am sure you have read these stories on the news. As a missionary and agent of the Gospel of Peace in this hard place, it disturbs me. We bring Bibles, food, books, love, songs, and the presence of the Lord Jesus, the Good News.

The gun is a toy, yes, of course, I know this Fred, but it is real in appearance. Lev was upset with me because I didn't bring the gun. Pasha spoke to Lev in an inappropriate way against me concerning this gun. He acted like another twelve-year-old boy, fussing because he couldn't have it. The enemy uses things just like this to divide and weaken our ministry. This was very hurtful and now causes more conflict between Pasha and I.

Fred, I understand that you want to give Lev presents. This helps the time and distance between you. I know how you miss him and want to do something to demonstrate your love. But Lev is still one of the boys of Lyahi orphanage. He told Valentina he didn't have to study him after you left over this.

We will return on Thursday to do another teaching session. Dima will begin working with us tomorrow. I know Lev will be looking to see what we are bringing him from you. If you would write him a letter, Fred, through my e-mail and support me in my decisions at this time, it will help him understand we have his best interests at heart.

We have already begun making plans for your summer camp. We will be looking forward to working with you and your team from July 1 to 15. Perhaps it will work out, Fred, that you could just come with the plan to stay through until your court. If we can get some kind of commitment from the adoptions center, it can be scheduled for early August.

Love in the Lord,

Jeanne

I was somewhat surprised at this letter because I didn't think Pasha was going to buy a gun for Lev that was a replica of a real gun. I thought Lev wanted a dart pistol that shoots darts at a target. A misunderstanding but one that could have caused problems. Of course, I didn't want Lev to walk around with a gun that could easily be mistaken for a real gun. So I wrote Lev a letter explaining to him that Jeanne had his best interest at heart and also that he should do nothing that may complicate the adoption. He needed to obey his teachers and the staff at the children's home so they wouldn't give him a bad report.

During the weeks of winter, it seemed as though nothing was happening, no progress. I knew I had to have patience and faith. My prayer life was growing as I surrendered to God my worries and doubts. I wanted desperately to believe there would be an adoption hearing in August with Lev coming home with me, but I had no assurance of this. I wrote another letter to Nadezhda thanking her for considering my petition, even though I wasn't sure she was. However, on February 19, 2001, I received a disturbing letter from Lev.

> Hello, my beloved daddy,
>
> This is your son Lev. Dad, I don't know where to start, either with good or bad. I have committed a great sin. I've ran away from the orphanage. And the teacher who works here had to do and find us with her own money. I very, very much ask you to forgive me, but I had to do this. I had to sell my player to pay back the money to a teacher. She said that we had to find money wherever we wanted to. Please forgive me. And in general, my behavior is not good, and I use words like stupid, etc. Skipping lessons in school. I don't know what's going on with me. I became so lazy. And there's this other thing that's the worst. I demand food pieces from a smaller kid. Dad, I ask you for forgiveness. I know it's a very ugly thing. I'm just a full stupid.
>
> I'm so afraid now that if I'll keep acting like that, they won't let me go to you. I'm giving you my honest word that I will correct myself. Honestly, Dad. Daddy, I miss you. You are my dear father. I can't wait for that moment when we will be together in our home. Well, I have to say good-bye. Please write back.
>
> I love you.
>
> PS: Hello from Vlad and me (Pasha). God bless you, bro. We pray for the situation. It all looks

like an attack from the devil. I still can't write from my computer. Maybe the Lord is taking it from me. I don't know. Well, tomorrow is a big day. Pray when we go to see Nadezhda Nikolayevna.

What I was seeing from these letters was a very frustrated boy who desperately wanted to be adopted, but it seemed like an eternity to him. When Lev ran away, he went to his deceased grandmother's flat, and the ladies renting it let him stay there for a few days. They then called the police and notified the orphanage to come and get him. He was not told all the legal challenges I was facing. He did not know that we were trying to get the courts to violate their rules on adoptions. There was no point in getting him even more frustrated than he already was. In all honesty, I did not know what was going to happen. I just knew that the Lord did not tell me to give up, and I would not give up without a clear understanding from the Lord.

I was so appreciative of the effort that Jeanne, Pasha, Dima, and others were making to bring this case to a positive conclusion. Without them, I don't know what I would have done. They were certainly a blessing to me. On March 22, 2001, Jeanne wrote:

Dear Fred,

I have a lot to share with you tonight. I sure do need your prayers, and I know you also covet ours. Please know we have been praying for you and these concerns. I received your dossier yesterday from the Draugh's. It was beautiful, Fred. As I held it, for me, there is a blessing on it. I could feel it, like it was anointed already and under the care of the Holy Spirit. An unbeliever probably won't notice, but then again?

I looked through it and found almost everything to be there. You did a really good job of putting it all together. I took it straight to Tonya last night, with the letter you had included to her. We had a long talk about the situation. She is going to keep it for the week and just think about the best thing to do with it. I told her your suggestion about coming back to talk to Nadezhda. Just pray about this. I had also thought about this last week.

When we went to Lyahi on Monday, I saw Lev just on the periphery, out of the corner of my eye. We were in the office with Valentina Milhaolvna talking about everything. When I came out of the office, Lev was standing out in the corner, with his ear to the window, out of sight of everyone but where he could hear. He did not come to the Bible study, and he would not come to speak with me. He sent a letter by Vlad's hand for me to translate and to send to you. He looked strained and has lost some weight.

Valentina says the court in Melinki still has not happened. "The judge is sick." Now, I understood in my spirit what is happening. The court will not pursue a hearing if it has not been approved by the center. It is now two months since the original scheduled date. For some reason, the Lord is postponing this necessary hearing. Valentina said, "Praise the Lord, it didn't happen on the first schedule day back in January. It was the day right after Lev had ran away. If it had gone to court that day, his chances for being adopted would have been finished that hour." Now the concern is the father is still in the picture. He is out of prison, but when the court does hear his case, if the father is anywhere around, they will not rule against him. This is what Tonya and Valentina tell me.

I asked Valentina and Tatiana about Lev coming out of the orphanage to stay with a family here in Vladimir until the adoption. They say no at this time. Until he has a court hearing and they place him on the registry, he cannot leave the orphanage for a long-term basis. Until the legal process has been completed, he cannot legally be eligible for adoption. If he comes out and then has to go back, it would be horrible, just horrible for him. I understand them and agree with them.

We understand the door is being squeezed shut by opposing forces. Last week was a strong meeting of the Department of Ministry. They issued strict instructions to all the orphanages that foreigners were no longer allowed to come or visit the orphanages without prior written approval of the Department of Education. Valentina told me about this. No teams, no visitors, no videos, pictures, etc. Plus, no help or food or blessings for the children. This was a major blow to me when I heard this. Well, praise the Lord for the relationships I already have with Tonya and others by the reputation of the work I have been doing here for the last

five years. Right there at ten o'clock in the evening, she called someone in the department and
asked about me. They had already heard about
me being closed out and said they would write
an exception for me, based on what has been
done in Lyahi during this time. We are praying
this will give us the legal authority to continue
to go there. Do you understand what is happening here, Fred?

I heard last night that international adop-
tions are being lobbied hard against in the
Duma. Tatiana says they are going to close the
door again. It is just a matter of a short time.
We know that no man can close the door except
God.

So she has your dossier, and I know she
is praying about the best way to go about pre-
senting it into Nadezhda's favor. Without her
approval, they won't even have Lev's court
in Melinki to have his father's parental right
removed. It is a delicate situation. I shared with
her that it is truly going to be a miracle from the
Lord's hand if it takes place. For us, we know he
is able and does miracles absolutely every minute of every day. We walk by faith, not by sight,
and we take heart in what we know about our
Lord, not what we see with our eyes. I asked her
to please help you because you are a dear friend
of mine and brother in the Lord. I begged her to
intercede for you. She will do what she can. As I
said earlier, I had thought to pray about several
times that you should consider coming back to

talk to Nadezhda in person and even to present to her yourself the translated dossier. We are not sure yet what is best and how to proceed. She does not like to be pressed. God will show us how to go.

Now here is the translated letter from Lev, dated March 19, 2001:

Dear Dad,
    I hope that now when you are reading this letter, everything is going well with you. Dad, please forgive me that I made you worry because of me. You ask why I ran away from the orphanage. I missed my former home. I've written former because now I have you, Daddy. Say hello to everybody in Florida from me. I'm looking forward to the moment when you take me home, Dad. I miss you very, very much. At night, before going to bed, I pray before the icon, and I pray for you too. Dad, I'll try my best to obey the teachers. Dad, I often dream that when you come to the camp, we'll go and pick mushrooms and berries, if only you will go with me. Dad, I've realized that the plastic pistol is a bad toy, and I don't need it. But this pistol costs much, and actually the money was wasted. I realize that you shouldn't have bought a pistol but should have brought the money here to the orphanage, and I would buy something sweet. Okay, let's forget about it. Sergey said hello to me, so say hello to him from me

please. Thank you that you are praying for me. Remember, Pasha told you that he bought me books to study English, and I traded them away. I know that I did wrong when I traded them. Please forgive me, Dad. I love you very much, my dear dad. I'm looking forward to getting your reply, and I'm waiting when you can come to me. Soon is my birthday. It's on the third of June.

Bye, in Jesus,
Son

From Jeanne on June 6, 2001:

Dear Fred,

Greetings to you in the Lord's dear name. Lev is doing great; he seems to have turned a corner in his walk with the Lord. He interacted well with the team and was present at the teachings.

June 25, 2001

Dear Fred,

We just returned from Lyahi. I had a list of things to accomplish today, and the Lord blessed us with victory. We saw Lev. He looks good—tanned, hair bleached blond from the sun. His court is tomorrow. *Praise the Lord.* His father showed up and is objecting to the adoption, but it is in the Lord's hands. The court will decide. It will go well; then while you are here, you can submit personally your letter of intent to adopt Lev directly to Nadezhda. If six months are required, he will be yours for Christmas. We have almost finished all the arrangements. Lots of details always to prepare for a team. We received permission from the mayor to do a "music-drama night" outreach on Thursday, July 5. We will print some invitations and have an afternoon to prayer walk and hand those out.

 We will meet you on Sunday with the bus as you return on the Delta flight. Thank you so much for praying for me personally. The Lord is faithful.

Jeanne

 Jeanne informed me that Lev finally had his day in court on June 27, 2001. His father was stripped of his parental rights. The judge was shocked that he hadn't bothered to go and see his son, even though he knew where he was. In fact, he hadn't seen Lev in ten years, had not written a letter, sent a card, purchased a gift or anything else. With this decision, Lev was placed on the adoption registry for six months. I agreed with Jeanne's decision that while I was in Russia for the summer camp, I could present myself to Nadezhda with my official letter of intent to adopt him.

CHAPTER 6

Second Summer Camp
July 1–15, 2001

Another summer camp was announced to Russia at the children's home for July 2001. This time, the church asked me to lead the trip. I was happy to do that, but there was a lot of work getting the team together: translators in Russia, making travel arrangements for about fourteen team members, etc. On this trip, Valentina, the orphanage director, invited the team to stay at the orphanage since the kids would be staying at the camp. It would be somewhat cramped and crowded, but we wouldn't have to travel twenty miles by bus every day to the campsite. She took two rooms—one for the ladies and one for the men—and set up cots for us. This arrangement saved us a lot of money that would have been spent on hotels. However, in the orphanage, there was no air-conditioning, and it was very hot. The windows did not have screening, so huge mosquitoes tortured us every night until we learned how to kill them before turning out the lights.

We knew most of the kids at this camp because most had been at the orphanage for years, and certainly they remembered us, even our names. We had come to love those kids. They were absolutely wonderful, and you wanted to take all of them out of there. The kids loved playing sports. We had brought a volleyball net and balls, along with soccer balls. They had no familiarity with baseball or American football, although we did introduce them to those sports. Swimming in the river was a big part of the afternoons when it was hot. There were quite a few rustic cabins that the kids slept in, not much different than those you see at American camps. The kids loved being at the camp far more than being in the orphanage building. Their total encampment would be six weeks. Three American churches sponsored and paid for six weeks of camp for the kids. The six weeks were split into three two-week periods with each church sending teams for each period. Without the church sponsorship, the kids would not have been able to go to such a nice camp like Camp Og, which was privately owned. The alternative would be for some of the kids to go to a government camp, which we were told was not very nice and many of the kids did not enjoy in the past.

We shopped for lots of food so the kids would eat well, and the cooks did a fantastic job in preparing the food. Most of the kids were quite skinny, although apparently healthy. I think by the time we left, they had all gained a few pounds.

I was able to spend a good deal of time with Lev during this encampment. He and I were really bonding as father and son. On the weekend in the middle of our encampment, Russia was celebrating a strange pagan fertility holiday called Ivan's Day (Ivan Kupala is the Russian name for John the Baptist.) He is considered the god of summer fertility. The celebration in this rural area included townspeople coming to the river at the camp and encouraging the kids to run around nude and even observe perfect strangers engaging in sexual activities. This caused a strain between Valentina and the team as we said we could not participate in such activities. Valentina said that they had participated in our Christian activities, and this was a cultural thing in Russia that that had been part of their rural life for many years. Rather than participate, we decided to leave the camp for the weekend and stay at a hotel in Vladimir, returning on Monday morning. Jeanne signed Lev out of camp, and we went back to Vladimir and spent the weekend at her flat while the other team members stayed at the hotel Zarya.

This gave Lev and I more time to bond. He took me all around Vladimir, showing me the building he used to live in when he was with his grand mom. We sat outside in the courtyard gazing at the building. We didn't know it at the time, but his grand mom had willed her flat to Lev. He was the owner of a four-room flat in down-town Vladimir. The location was fantastic, with a soccer stadium right across the street, and all the stores and businesses of downtown were just outside the door. At that time, we had no idea what had happened to her possessions. While we were sitting in the courtyard, one of the old ladies came out of the building and recognized Lev. She hugged him and said how sorry she was that his grand mom had died as they were friends. He told her who I was, and she hugged me and asked me to be sure and take care of him. She said that two ladies were living in his grand mom's flat, and all her possessions were still there.

I really enjoyed getting to know the city of Vladimir. It is a very old city with walls over a thousand years old. The Kremlin was there at one time. Downtown Vladimir, where Lev used to live, is fascinating. It was obvious that the city was starting to come back from hard times. They were building new restaurants and hotels. The first bowling alley had just opened along with a Chinese restaurant next to it. Public transportation in Russia is excellent. Buses, trolleys, and jitneys are continuously traveling up and down the main streets. You never have to wait more than a few minutes for transportation, and it's very cheap. I believe a bus ticket was about ten cents. In the largest cities, such as Moscow and St. Petersburg, subways are the primary mode of transportation. On almost every corner, there are flower stalls with some of the most beautiful fresh flowers available, and fresh baked bread is available every day from the street kiosks. The bread is heavy and delicious and warm from just coming out of the ovens. Monday morning, we all went back to Lyahi to the camp and finished out the second week. We were in some ways expecting a look of disapproval from Valentina and the staff when we returned, but there was nothing but smiles.

I decided to take a quick break from the camp to visit Nadezhda in Vladimir. I just had to know what was going on. I prayed that God would give me favor with Nadezhda. I put on a suit and tie, and I asked another Russian friend, Lena, who speaks excellent English, to be my translator when I went to see Nadezhda. Lena was able to get us an appointment, and we went to the office on the date and time set. Nadezhda did not speak English, and I did not speak Russian, so a translator was necessary. We sat in the hallway of the office for about an hour before Nadezhda came out to greet us. Before she came out, I prayed, and I felt God wanted me open my Bible, which I had with me to Proverbs 21:1: "The king's heart is like a stream of water directed by the Lord; he turns it wherever he pleases." After reading that, all my apprehension and nervousness disappeared. I truly felt this meeting would be in God's hands, and he would turn it wherever he pleased. My first impression of Nadezhda was not good. She had a very harsh look on her face. I'm sure she was not happy to see me in any case since she had let me know in no uncertain terms that I did not meet the qualifications for adoption in Russia.

Nadezhda had me sit down and immediately started questioning me on why I should be allowed to adopt a Russian child in violation of the rules. She reiterated that according to Russian rules, I was too old to adopt, and in any case, they did not permit single people to adopt. Actually, I had looked up Russian adoption law on the Internet and saw that their constitution did not forbid single folks from adopting, but I didn't think it wise to say that to her. This was just something that the agencies adopted as a rule. Jeanne also said that she didn't think it was illegal for singles to adopt. However, Nadezhda said that she saw no reason to violate the rules. Russia is all about rules (and stamps). I have never seen so many things that need official stamps on them as I did in Russia. I shared with her that I did not come to Russia with the intent to adopt a child. It was the furthest thing from my mind. However, after spending two weeks in the orphanage and developing a fondness for Lev, I went home and asked several of my friends if they would adopt him as I really wanted to see him leave the orphanage. I told her that as I pleaded with friends, who probably were qualified to adopt, they all kept saying to me that since I knew this boy, I should adopt him. I told them that I didn't feel that I wanted to adopt a child, but this was a fine boy, and he would be a great addition to someone's home. Over and over again, they insisted that I adopt him. At that time, I did not know what the rules for adoption were in Russia. I did not know that they preferred folks under age fifty, and I didn't know that single adults were prohibited from adopting. I shared all these with Nadezhda, and it didn't seem to move her. She asked me if I had kept in communication with Lev, and I said yes. I told her that this was my third trip to the orphanage, and Lev and I had become very close. I don't know why, but I had brought all the letters that Lev and I had exchanged and showed them to her. Thankfully, the original letters were in Russian, which she could read. While she was reading the letters, I showed her the many photos I had of Lev and I at the camps. She saw in the letters how fond Lev was of me and his desire to leave the orphanage. As Nadezhda was reading the letters, I observed her countenance changing. Not only did she read the letters once, she reread them. Maybe it was my imagination, but she appeared to be changing right before my eyes. Her countenance went from harshness to that of a kindly grandmother. She asked me if she could make copies of the letters, and of course, I said yes. She went out of the room and came back several minutes later and handed me the original letters back. She then proceeded to ask me about my home and job and also about my family back in the US. I don't know why, but a complete peace enveloped me. I saw warmth in her that I didn't see before. Finally, she said, "Mr. Ragsdale, I shouldn't be doing this; it is certainly against the rules, but I am going to forward your application over to the courts. I do not make the decision on whether you can adopt; only a court can do that. My job is to make sure all the qualifications are met. I don't know what the judges will do with your application, but why don't we see." At that, I thanked her profusely, shook her hand, and gave her a box of chocolates. I wanted to kiss her but thought it best not to. It is customary to give gifts to officials in Russia when they assist you beyond what they have to do. She thanked me, and I left her office. To say I was full of hope would be an understatement. I felt that I had just witnessed another miracle of God.

What an absolute blessing those two weeks were. All the team members wished we could stay longer, but unfortunately, we had to leave and go home. Leaving Lev behind was especially difficult this time. Next to the last day of our stay at the camp, Lev who was usually very happy and cheerful, was very sullen and at times was sitting on the floor crying. I sat with him and asked him what was wrong. He wouldn't say anything, just kept looking at the floor. I asked a staff member if she knew what was wrong with Lev. She said, "He is extremely sad that you are leaving and he isn't going with you." I felt crushed. I wanted to snatch him up and somehow get him out of there, although I knew I would have to wait until everything was legal, and that would be no sooner than December or January. It just seemed to be taking so long. Now, it was a year since I first tried to adopt him, and I felt we were no closer to the finish line. I got a translator to sit with me and Lev, and I tried to explain to him that he would be adopted, but we had to wait until Russia permitted it and that I would not abandon him under any circumstances. I hugged him tightly to try and reassure him. On our last day, Lev seemed to be back to his normal happy self until we all got on the bus. All the kids surrounded the bus to wave good-bye. Lev was standing beside the bus gazing in the window with tears coming down his cheeks. I tried to smile through my tears. It actually hurt to leave him there, especially not knowing what was going to happen.

In the meantime, I completed the adoption training that was required and additional paper work needed by the adoption agency. I figured that the adoption would take place in January or February 2002. Knowing that Nadezhda was behind our case helped me feel pretty good about the outcome, although the waiting seemed interminable. The church was sending another team to Lyahi for a second winter holiday camp. I wasn't sure whether to sign up or not since it was possible that the adoption case may come up around the same time. I got an e-mail from Nadezhda that my adoption court case would be held on January 5, 2002. Derek and Clair Klein, teammates and friends from Tampa who were adopting three children, had their case set for January 2, 2002. I was pretty happy and decided to go on the holiday camp trip, which would have me in Russia on January 5. I was to leave Tampa on December 29, arriving in Moscow on December 30, 2001.

On November 12, 2001, I received another letter from Jeanne:

Dear Fred,
I think you must be so busy right now, and there is too much stress going on in your life. Know that I am praying for you. As I spoke to Tatiana, she asked for some of those hook rug forms like you sent earlier. They love those things, and it is a good craft for the older girls. If you could bring a few more as a gift, it will be a big blessing for them. I went straight into the education building to use our new bath-

rooms, and when I came down the steps, Lev was standing by. Lord, Fred, he is looking just wild. He wouldn't speak to me. I tried everything I knew to get any response from him. He is rude and almost mean there. He looks dirty and ragged. Lena was with me, and she is very sensitive to the spirit. He handed me a letter, and I gave him yours. I was unable to get any eye contact with him whatsoever. He just stood there staring out the window, clenching his teeth. I saw him later in the cafeteria. He was huddled in the corner, hunched over his bowl of soup, sitting by himself. He refused to come around any of us. Wouldn't come to the lesson. I thought Dima might be able to minister to him, but Lev wouldn't have it. Lena and I prayed for him, and both of us felt like there is some gross shame all over him. I fear what has happened to him there. I asked Tatiana about him, and she said he is not going to do anything else until you come. But in the meantime, they are requiring him to obey and go to school, so there are some big conflicts there for him. He runs away and fights with the other boys. I have attached the letter Lev gave me for you:

Hello, my dearest daddy,

This is your dear son writing to you. Daddy, I didn't know where to start, from the bad or from the good. Okay, let's start with the bad things and finish with the good.

Fred, I have very bad behavior. I am not listening to the teachers. I am leaving without permissions and skipping lessons, and most importantly, I am forgetting about Jesus and God.

Daddy, now I will tell you how they punish me for skipping lessons. Remember where you stayed when you were here last winter? So I live in this building right now. Near with this building is the cafeteria and bedroom upstairs. So this cafeteria where you ate, they force me to wash it all week. It was very hard for me to clean it. Other guys also skip lessons, but nobody forced them to wash for the whole week. Everything you gave me as a present I have sold or lost. Also, the teachers told me you will refuse me. If this is true, please write to me about it. Daddy, please write to me everything about adoptions. How it is going. All the bad things are finished. Sorry, please forgive me. How are you doing? How is work? What is the weather like?

The days we spent together, I remember them very often. I laugh for a long time. Well, this is it, and I wanted to tell you. I'm sorry that I didn't write to you for a long time. I wait for your letter for when you can come to get me, Daddy.

With all my heart,
Your loving son.

Good-bye, Papa

I knew from all the correspondence from Jeanne, Pasha, and even Lev that he was in deep trouble emotionally. What was going on was difficult for me but was simply too much for a young boy who had suffered so much loss in his life to bear. I knew I had to get him out of that orphanage. I felt his very life was in danger, or if he kept acting out, he could be sent to a juvenile detention home, which would finish him off.

A Letter from Jeanne on October 1, 2001:

Dear Fred,

The cold weather is coming fast. It is thirty-two today with a wind. We have two weeks to go before they will turn on the heat, so remember to pray for us. I am always glad to hear from you. I appreciate your heart and care so very much. We went to Lyahi on Thursday. It was the first time I had been there in six weeks. Valentina and Tatiana were there, and we had about an hour to sit and talk about everything. The Holy Spirit was so strong during our meeting. I began to speak about the love of the Lord for us and His faithfulness, even during the hardest times. Her eyes shed tears, and the presence of the Lord was strong in the room. We received permission to return for our teachings, and she even suggested we come on Sunday afternoon so that all the children could attend and the staff too! This was straight from the Lord as far as I was concerned. It seemed the next season opening will be "church" there in the orphanage for all the children. We are praying now about the details. I have a meeting tomorrow with Pastor Jeff to discuss this and other things with him.

Going unannounced this time was good too because I could see how things really are there, and they are *not* good. The children are looking gray and stressed again. They had almost *no* food! It was terrible, Fred. They had soup that was just water and a few fragments of fish (a piece about the size of your fingernail)! *No* kidding. We were just grossing out, and I realized how bad off they are again.

I saw Lev right away and gave him your letter. Velodia spent a little time with him. His is depressed and so sad. He worries me, and I fear for him. He is just living for the day when you will come, and for him right now, he is getting so worn down waiting. You could just see his desperate look in his eyes. My field pastor from Poland was with me on this visit. He has the gift of intercession and strong spiritual discernment. We went to Lev and laid hands on him in prayer. Gary prayed for him twice more during his visit. Lev sent a letter, and I will follow with it. Fred, is it possible you could come and stay for the weeks after camp until your court? Just a thought.

Tatiana mentioned to me that Nadezhda was not pressing your case, and you will need to go and see her again when you come. If you were here, you could go and strongly request a hearing the first day the courts resume. Lynn should be your strong advocate in this, Fred.

She has Natasha, who is actually working inside the adoption center here in Vladimir.

Today, we bought two hundred forty kilograms of meat, two hundred kilograms of rice, two hundred kilograms of enriched wheat, yeast, and one hundred kilograms of enriched macaroni to take this evening. We are going to contract with a dairy in Melinki to provide milk and curds to them twice weekly. I am spending "faith" funds to be able to do this, but I cannot turn my back on all these hungry children there I love.

Kolya has gone to the Kilchugina region. He stole some more stuff from the staff before he left, says Tatiana.

Dear brother, thank you for the prayers you pray from my joy and peace. I am pressing on to take hold of the prize.

Love to you, in the Lord,
Jeanne

A Letter from Lev on October 1, 2001:

My dear Fred,

I was very glad to get your letter through Jeanne. I'll tell you how I'm doing. I can say I live all right; my health is okay. I go to school, and I've started to get better there. I think Vlad wrote you how I behaved in the beginning of the school year. We quarreled with him because of it. I am sorry and worried about what happened in your country in New York and Washington. Now I go to an old lady and help her. When you come, I'll introduce you to her. Write how your health is, your work, and how you are.

Say hello to your friends from me. That's all. Good-bye, Dad.

Love and kisses,
Your loving son

I'm looking forward to your coming, and I'm counting days till we see each other again and are together. Bye.

On December 28, I got an e-mail from Nadezhda stating that the court case was good for the Tampa couple but that the case for Ragsdale was cancelled. There would be no court hearing for Lev and me. "Oh my god, no!" This news sent shockwaves of disbelief through me. I fell on my knees, asking God to tell me why. How could you let me come this far to leave me? This will kill Lev, as he is so eager. What do I do? There was no reason given in the notice. Not even, "We're sorry." I felt traumatized, helpless, and very, very upset.

CHAPTER 7

Going Back to Russia

December 2001

Packing for this trip to Russia was just awful. I wanted to see Lev, but I had no idea how I would explain to him what had happened, that our dreams had been crushed, and he would have to stay in the orphanage. It would be devastating news. Going to the Tampa airport was not filled with the usual joy in embarking on a wonderful trip. I felt like I was going to a funeral. I could not bear to see Lev's look of total disappointment that I imagined he would have. How could I tell him that this God of love we had been preaching about was going to deny him the right to be adopted? Would he lose his faith in God? I was spending a lot of time praying and begging God to intervene. How would I be able to be joyful during this holiday camp when I felt so defeated? I felt that God was telling me that it wasn't over until he said it was over and to not give up hope. I felt him telling me not to tell Lev that the dream was dead because God was still on his throne and to remember he directs the hearts of men as he chooses. This lifted me up.

I was traveling separately from the other team members. I had made arrangements to be picked up in Moscow by my friend Pasha and then driven to the orphanage in Lyahi. There was one major problem: my visa to enter Russia had not yet come in from the Russian Embassy in Washington. Without the visa, there would be no trip. I had sent the application in plenty of time and included a self-addressed priority mail envelope for them to use to get it back to me. To get a Russian visa, one has to send his passport with an official invitation from Russia to the embassy in Washington, and they attach the visa to the passport and return it. I hate sending my passport to the embassy, but there is no other way. My passport and visa should have arrived more than a week before I left. As time got closer for departure, I started calling the embassy to find out what had happened to my visa. The person who answered the phone told me that my visa had been approved and mailed out days before; however, I did not receive it. Two days before departure, I called the embassy again, and they continued to tell me that it had been mailed over a week before, and they had no idea why I hadn't received it. My heart started sinking as I thought maybe it was lost in the mail. But how? It was in a large priority mail envelope. I even went to my local post office and asked the clerk to check to see if it was there. Nothing. She told me to come back later in the day and check to see if it had come in the late mail. I went back in the afternoon, but there was no mail for me. Now I was in complete distress. What else can go wrong? If the visa didn't come to the post office overnight and I could not pick it up as soon as they opened, I would not be able to go. I would be completely sunk. Believing that the visa had to be in the morning mail and believing that God would not fail me at this point, I went to the post office in much hope. When I walked into the post office, the same clerk that had been waiting on me before told me to wait while she went in the back to check. I had previously told her what I was waiting on, so she knew what to look for. She came back out to the counter and sadly told me that it had not arrived, and she was very sorry knowing that my trip was now over. I walked out of the post office with tears in my eyes and saying, "What's next, Lord? Have I been defeated by the forces of darkness? I felt my air ticket was now worthless. (The ticket was not actually worthless. I could change the dates for a fee and go on a later date). Was this your will all along? I am completely undone." I went home, sat down at my computer, and e-mailed Pasha, telling him that I would not be coming because my visa didn't arrive in time. I took my luggage back in the bedroom and started unpacking, meanwhile trying to make sense of what has happened. A few minutes later, my doorbell rang. I went to the door, and it was the clerk from the post office. She came in her *own car* to my house to deliver the priority mail envelope with my passport and visa. It had just come in, and she knew how important it was (bless you, postal employees). This was an incredible miracle. I never expected this to happen in a thousand years. I could not have planned it. I started thanking God, but I also knew I had absolutely no time to waste if I was to catch my flight to New York, which was scheduled to leave at ten thirty that morning. Since it was already nine o'clock in the morning, I could not imagine how I could repack, drive to the airport, park in the garage, get in the terminal, get my boarding pass, go through security, and make it to the plane before it departed. I prayed, "God, please help me make this flight." Also, how would Pasha now know I am coming? (I don't have time to e-mail him.) "Lord, I need another of your miracles." Tampa International Airport is about twenty-five minutes from my house if there are no traffic backups on the bridge over Tampa Bay. This was going to be impossible unless there was another miracle. I got a flash in my brain. My friend Cezar lived halfway between my house and the airport. If I could drive to his house, then have him take me to the airport and take my car back to his house, that would shave off precious minutes. Since his house was just off the interstate, it would not be out of my way. Now, please be home. I called him, and he answered his home phone. I told him what I needed him to do, and he said, "No problem, I'll be waiting outside for you." I threw clothes back in my suitcases and then drove like a maniac to Cezar's house. He was waiting outside the door as he had said. I jumped out and switched to the passenger side, and he started driving toward the airport. Even with this, I knew I was dangerously close to missing the flight. I decided to call Delta Airlines and ask them to hold the plane as I was on my way. Do they even do that? Now, for another miracle. I have never called an airline and had a human answer on the first ring without going through a large menu of choices. I called; an actual agent answered the phone on the first ring. I explained that I was on the Howard Frankland Bridge, minutes from the airport (like they would know where that was), and would be at the gate as soon as I could get my boarding pass and make it through security. The agent who answered the phone said, "Mr. Ragsdale, don't worry about making that flight. It has been cancelled due to a major snowstorm in New York. We have already booked you on tomorrow's flight through New York to Moscow." I couldn't believe what she was saying. I had not given her my name. How did she know it was me who was calling? We were now in the airport. Cezar made a turn through the airport, and we went back to his house. It's funny, but all along, I felt that I was forgetting to pack some necessary items, and I could not remember if I even locked my door. When I got home, I realized that I had not locked my front door, and I had forgotten to pack shoes and long underwear for the trip.

The next day, I was able to pack properly, lock my doors, and drive leisurely to the airport. I had e-mailed Pasha and told him I would be coming, only a day later than planned. He would send my other friend Dima to the airport to pick me up. In one of my suitcases, I had packed about forty vials of donated penicillin for the orphanage nurse. She said that she had no antibiotics to treat infections with and couldn't obtain any from the official pharmacy in town. Some doctors in the US gave me the medicines to give to her.

In all the times I had gone through customs at Moscow airport, never did they ask me to open any of my luggage. I always went through the line that said "Nothing to Declare." This time I was stopped by the customs agent, and she pointed to the suitcase with the penicillin and asked me to open it. I opened the bag, and as soon as she saw the vials of penicillin, which were lying on top of my clothes, she said coldly, "This not allowed in Russia. You go to jail." I said, "What?" She asked me if I had papers for the penicillin, and I said that I didn't. She repeated, "You go to jail." I was totally petrified, thinking that here I was alone in Moscow airport and I was going to be carted off to jail. I decided I had to do something drastic. For whatever stupid reason, I decided to run. I ran out of the immigration area almost waiting to get shot in the back. I saw my friend Dima, and I ran over to him and yelled that they were ready to put me in jail for bringing in penicillin. I told him he had to come back into the immigration area to talk to the officer. I dragged him back into an area banned for nonpassengers (he could have been arrested). He started talking frantically to the agent in Russian. I didn't know what they were saying, so I just started praying. Finally, she said, "Okay, you don't go to jail. I just fine you. Put it up on the scale." I started taking the penicillin out of the case to put on the scale. She said, "No, the whole suitcase." It weighed, according to her, eighteen kilos. She fined me four dollars per kilo, which came out to seventy-two dollars. I had to walk around the airport to find the police station where I could pay my fine. When I went back to the immigration area to retrieve my luggage, I gave her the receipt, and she let me take the luggage with the penicillin in it. I felt like this should have been videotaped. Afterward, we all got a good laugh out of it, but it wasn't funny during the time, and my knees were still shaking,

When I got to Moscow, they were going through an unbeliev-able cold spell. Temperatures were ten to thirty degrees below zero with heavy winds. There was snow everywhere. For someone who just left Florida with temperatures in the midseventies, it was absolutely bone-chilling.

The drive from Moscow to Lyahi is about seven hours in good weather with no snow on the ground. Today, this drive seemed to take forever. Valentina was gracious to let the team stay at the orphanage. When I saw Lev, it seemed like he had grown several inches since the last time. He seemed so tall, although still skinny. We hugged, and the first thing he said through the translator was "Are you here to take me home?" I died a little inside. I couldn't tell him that our court date had been cancelled. So I just told him to have patience; we're still waiting for the Russian officials to give their permission. He seemed okay with that. I spent a few days with Lev and the other kids at the orphanage. We played in the snow although I was dying from the cold. I called Lena Shagin-Rayeva who lived in Vladimir and asked her if she could meet me the next day in Vladimir, come to Nadezhda's office, and translate for me. I needed desperately to see her and find out what had happened. Lena said she could do that. Jeanne's driver, Vlad, took me on the three-hour drive to Vladimir, the capital of that region. We met at Lena's flat and then drove over to the adoption office. I had not made an appointment because I didn't want Nadezhda to refuse to meet with me. I would just go in and ask to speak with her. When we entered the building, Nadezhda was in the hallway, and she saw me come in. She walked right over to me and shook my hand, which kind of took me by surprise. She told us that it wasn't she who cancelled the court hearing. The judges refused to hear the case because it did not meet Russian rules on adoptions. She took us in her office, and she tried to give me comfort as she could see how desperately disappointed I was. I could see she really cared. She again told me that she cannot force the judges to hear a case as that is their prerogative, and they are just following established rules. My case was outside the rules, and they were not going to set a new precedent. Nadezhda asked me if I would be willing to take Lev to the US for educational purposes only. I could be his foster parent for up to five years. She could probably get that approved. It would be short of an actual adoption, and at the end of five years, he would have to return to Russia. I told her there was no way I could bring Lev home with me and then at the end of five years send him back to Russia. It would kill me and him. (I was reminded of what my adoption agency director Lynn had told me—that they had been doing successful adoptions in Russia for years and were absolutely convinced that I would not be successful.) I thought, am I just being foolish? Here I am five thousand five hundred miles from home in a very foreign country hoping and praying they will violate their own rules for me and Lev. I recalled God telling me that it's not over until he says it's over. Was God now telling me it's over?

We sat quietly in Nadezhda's office absorbing defeat. How do I tell Lev? How do I tell all the folks back home who are praying for us? How do I go back to the orphanage with a smile on my face? I hadn't even been able to tell folks that the court case had been cancelled. How do I even settle my own heart? Should I reconsider being a foster parent for five years and hope things would change? I just wanted to crawl into a ball on the floor and cry, realizing that yes, it was over. The fight was over. But then I realized again that God had told me it wasn't over until he said it was over. (I had a memory of a business trip to Chicago with one of my co-workers, and while there, we went to a blues club, and when I thought the show was over, he said, "It's not over until the fat lady sings." I thought that was just an expression until a very fat lady got up and finished out the show with some amazing songs.) I said very softly, "God, is it over? Has the fat lady sung? I need to hear from you." Just then, Nadezhda said to me, "Can you come back to Russia in a month?" She continued, "I will send your file back to the courts, and maybe different judges will look at it and at least approve a hearing." I said, "Of course, I will come back." She said that even though it would be a violation of her own office procedures, she would set a court date for February 11 and send the paperwork to the court. For some reason, I felt I needed to hug this woman who was doing something that could get her in trouble. I gave her a big Russian bear hug, and she hugged me back. Hope was back in the air. I went back to the orphanage and told Lev that he would be leaving in February. "God, please let this be true. I know you haven't taken me this far to leave me." I came back to Florida with hope back in my heart. The fat lady hadn't sung yet. I made plans and bought a ticket to return to Russia for a February 11 court date. I got on my knees and prayed, and I said to God, "I'm not going to buy just my ticket; I'm buying a ticket for Lev to come home. I'm buying it in faith. I'm buying it knowing that you are faithful and you didn't carry me this far to leave me. Lev is my son, and he is coming home."

I purchased a roundtrip ticket for me and a one-way ticket for Lev. Thankfully, on the previous trip, I had acquired a double-entry visa and would not need to get one for this trip. Why I did that at the time, I don't know, but it sure was helpful. I guess that was another miracle from God. My faith was now not in the Russian system but squarely in God's promise. I waited, but I did not get an e-mail telling me the case was cancelled, which was good, so on February 8, I boarded a flight to Moscow. On the plane, I prayed to God, saying, "Please, God, don't let this trip be in vain. Please don't let this be a fool's mission. If you never do anything for me again, let this boy come home with me."

I was aware that the ability of foreigners to adopt Russian children was on very shaky ground. President Vladimir Putin had demonstrated his dislike of Americans. The Russian Duma was repeatedly submitting bills to ban adoptions of Russian children by foreigners, especially Americans. I was praying not to get caught up in that trap. So far, none of the bills had passed, but I was warned that it was just a matter of time, maybe just days, because they were gaining support. News reports of Russian children being abused by their American parents and even killed were especially troubling to the Russian legislators, and they made a big news on Russian TV. Even the adoption agencies were convinced that adoptions might come to a screeching halt in the very near future. This was just one more thing for me to worry about. If they passed one of these bills before my adoption was finalized, it would be dead in the water, and all my efforts would be in vain. But my trust was not in the Russian Duma or President Putin but in the Lord. And he said, "It's not over until I say it's over."

CHAPTER 8

Court

I arrived in Russia on February 9, 2002, with my emotions all over the place. Part of me was joyous believing that God was going to bring this adoption to completion. At other times, I would get somewhat depressed, allowing Satan to convince me I was on a fool's errand. Outside the international arrivals area, I met my driver Vlad who was going to take me to Vladimir. When we left the airport, I was shocked at how warm it was outside. It was February, in the middle of winter, and it was warm enough that I did not even need to zip up my coat. Just the month before, it was unbelievably cold. Was this a sign? We drove the three hours to Vladimir, and I signed in to my hotel. I called Lena and asked her to call the adoption office to see if the hearing was still scheduled. It was. Lena came by the hotel, and we went to the courthouse on the 11, arriving in time for the one o'clock in the afternoon hearing. Courts are very formal in Russia. I was told that adoption cases usually take less than two hours. I was surprised that they had a prosecutor who would be arguing for the court to deny the adoption. Why? I wondered. Valentina, the orphanage director, was there as it was she who brought Lev to court and she would have to give her recommendation. Also present was a representative from the education department and one from the Agency for Adoptions, Custody, and Guardianship. There was a court stenographer who was writing in long hand, not on a stenotype machine. Wow. How antiquated. I guess she was using shorthand because she seemed to keep up with the proceedings. (Once, court was halted while the stenographer went out to get another pad to write on.) There were other people in the courtroom, and I had no idea who they were. Lev and I were told to sit in a side section at the front of the courtroom. We were assigned an official court translator who was translating between English and Russian and vice versa for my benefit. Without her, I would not have understood anything, as everything spoken was in Russian. Lev understood the Russian, and I understood the English. Before court started, the translator came over and introduced herself and told me that she does this on a regular basis whenever American or other English-speaking folks are in the court and need that service. She asked me about myself and how my name was pronounced. She did want to give me a warning. She asked me if I was a Christian, and I said I was. She said please don't blurt that out to the judge. Most of the judges are atheists and consider Christians weak and sometimes will use that as a reason to deny the adoption. I told her there was no reason for me to say anything about my religious beliefs unless I was asked. She said, "The judge won't ask you, but in the past, some Christian couples have blurted out that they felt that Jesus was telling them to adopt a Russian child, and this very much offends the judges." I told her that I wouldn't be doing that and she shouldn't worry.

A few minutes later, Judge Samylov came in, and everyone stood while court was brought in session. I tried to determine what kind of man the judge was by his appearance. Was he a kind man? A decent man? A fair man? He was tall, middle-aged, with a somewhat stern expression on his face. I couldn't tell what kind of person he was. He showed no emotion, and he never smiled. People don't often smile publicly in Russia. Even though the translator was reciting in English what was going on, much of the process was unfamiliar to me. Lev was sitting beside me, and he seemed nervous and somewhat apprehensive. They read off my request to adopt this child, noting that the child was free to be adopted and that no relative or Russian family had shown interest in adopting him. They said that the six-month waiting period had been observed. They said that his biological father's parental rights had been terminated in a previous hearing. Then the prosecutor got up and stated his reasons why Lev should not be allowed to be adopted and sent to America. He said that Lev should serve his country in the armed forces when he was older and that he could have a good future in Russia. Valentina, the orphanage director, was called to the stand and asked if she knew me and if she thought I would make a good father for Lev. She was very generous in her praise, saying that I had been to the orphanage many times on church mission trips, and she felt I would make a great father for Lev. I noticed the judge picked up the words "mission trips," and that made me wonder if that was going to be a problem for us, him knowing that church mission trips were most likely Christian. He didn't say anything at that time. The court called me to the stand, and the judge started asking me questions, many questions. "Where did I live? How much did I pay for my house? How much do I make? What other children do I have at home? Where do I work? What do I do? Why did I divorce?" Question after question. Then Lev was called to the stand. He was questioned about whether he was aware that if he was adopted, he may never come back to "his" country again. He was asked about his life in the orphanage and why he wanted to be adopted. He gave great answers telling the judge that he wanted a family again. He said that the only family member who cared about him was his grandmother and that she had died, and he had no one in Russia who cared about him. He told the judge he definitely wanted to be adopted by me.

This hearing had been going on over three hours, and it appeared that the judge needed to end it for the day, so he told all of us to be back in the courtroom tomorrow at nine o'clock in the morning. Lev and Valentina had to drive the three hours in the snow back to Lyahi, and I just had to go a few blocks to my hotel. This was definitely taking longer than anyone had thought, but there was nothing I could do but follow the judge's orders and come back tomorrow, Thursday, February 12.

We returned to the courthouse on Thursday. I still had no idea how things would turn out. The translator came up to me and said it was the longest adoption hearing she had attended. The judge took his seat on the bench, and court came to order. I was called back to the stand for more questions. My brain was spinning, and I started feeling ill. I said a quick prayer that God would give me strength to deal with whatever was coming. Then it was Lev's turn to be asked more questions. After about two hours of questioning, the judge asked Lev what he would do with his life if he disapproved the adoption request. What fourteen-year-old knows what he is going to do with his life? Lev looked stunned. However, he answered that he would stay in the orphanage until he finished school and then would probably end up in the army. I saw a look of despondency come over Lev's face. I was then summoned to the stand. The judge asked me what I would do if he disapproved the petition. I said that I would stay in Lev's life and do all I could to see that he knew someone loved him and cared for him. I would visit him as often as I could. The judge then, without warning, asked me if I believed in God. I could see the blood drain out of the translator's face as she relayed the question to me. It seemed as if she was praying I would say no. I said yes. He then said, "Do you talk to this boy about God?" I said, "Yes." He said, "What do you say to him about God?" The interpreter was shaking as she translated his words. I was thinking, *I guess Lord this is it. He's got me. I'm trapped.* However, I do have a choice. I can deny a belief in God or I can admit my belief and lose the case. But I refuse to come all this way to deny God no matter the consequences. I said to the judge, "I tell Lev that God is our Father in heaven and that he sent his only begotten son, Jesus, to the earth to redeem man from his sin. That those who place their faith in him and believe in him will inherit eternal life and those who don't will go to hell." The judge stared at me almost in disbelief, but he didn't say anything. I started thinking maybe all this was for me to stand in a Russian courtroom and deliver the Gospel to unbelieving folks. Instead of being afraid of the consequences (losing Lev), I felt energized. The judge called for the courtroom to be cleared, and everyone left except his staff. I went out into the anteroom. The translator came out totally shaken up. She said that in all her times in the courtroom, she had never seen a judge ask such a question. She said that it probably would not go well for me. She then told us that if we are out of the courtroom for an hour, it means that the adoption is being approved. However, if twenty minutes or less, that's a sign that it is going to be denied. They don't waste a lot of time on denials. We were out for ten minutes, and they called us back in to the courtroom. The judge started reading Russian law as it pertains to adoption. He said adoption was not for the benefit of the adopting parents or for their enjoyment but solely for the benefit of the child. It was his duty to ensure that the best interests of the child were served. He said that after listening to all the testimony and looking at the facts before him, it was his opinion that the best interest of Lev Migalinski was to approve his adoption to Frederick Ragsdale. When the interpreter told me what he said, I came absolutely unglued. I was so ready to hear "petition denied." I couldn't believe it. I felt God saying quietly to me, "Now it's over, my son." Lev and I hugged for a long time. I never believed until that final moment that the judge would rule in our favor. I spent the next few minutes in the courtroom hugging everybody— Valentina, Lena, and others who had put their faith in me. It was such a joyous moment. Finally, Judge Samylov came down off the bench and approached us. He stretched out his hand, and speaking in English for the first time, he said, "Mr. Ragsdale, I know this was an ordeal for you and Lev, but I needed to make sure since this was outside Russian rules for this region that I could justify my decision if I decided in your favor. I congratulate you for convincing the court of your ability to be a good father for this boy. Not only will you be a fine father but, most of all, I am most thankful that you believe in God. Please bring this boy up to know the Lord. I am suspending the rule that you remain in Russia for ten days. You can go back to the United States whenever you complete your documents. I will sign all orders that you need to change his name or anything else. Thank you for what you are doing for this boy." I thanked him profusely for his ruling and promised him I would be the best father I could be. I couldn't help the tears welling up in my eyes. Thank you, God.

It was then that I realized that the judge must have been a Christian. Is that why the Lord had me come back to Russia? To stand before a Christian judge rather than an atheist judge? Wow, how do we fathom the hand of the Lord? From the courthouse, I called the adoption agency in Chicago and told them the result. They started screaming, "Oh my god, you're the first! You're the first single man to successfully adopt in Russia." One of the things I realized was that my being a black American had no impact on the decision. No one, and I mean no one in Russia treated me with anything but respect, whether in a hotel, restaurant, store, church, etc. Eventually, I saw some other persons of color. I saw a young black man working as a sales clerk in a downtown Vladimir store, and I saw several others working in the city. They were Russian black people who only spoke Russian for the most part. On one of my flights from Russia back to the US, I sat next to a middle-aged black lady on the plane. When the flight attendant was handing out newspapers, I took a *USA Today*, and she took a Russian-language newspaper. I asked her if she read Russian, and she said yes. Through conversation, I found out she was born in Moscow but had been working in Chicago for the public school system, helping Russian immigrants to Chicago adapt to American life. She said that she was about to retire from the system after twenty-five years, and I asked her where she would live in retirement. She answered that she would be living in Russia. I asked why, and she said that black people in Russia face no discrimination such as they do in the United States. She feels free to do anything she wants, but only when she is in the US is she acutely aware of her race. She told me that there are quite a few black people who have been born and raised in Russia. They are remnants of slavery in the US in the eighteenth century when many blacks fled the US for Europe. Many settled in Russia, and they were treated well. Russia has no history of black slavery, and the blacks there are treated as regular Russian citizens. I was shocked to say the least, but it answered my concern about whether my race would have any impact on the adoption. It didn't in Russia, but it certainly did in the US.

Lev standing next to orphanage director Valentina Milhaolvna and Tatyana Volkova (far left) in the hallway of the courthouse in Vladimir, February 2012

Tatyana, Valentina and Fred in courthouse for adoption proceeding

CHAPTER 9

Thank God for Lena

I cannot thank God enough for Lena. Without her, I don't know how I would have navigated all the offices that were required in order to obtain all the documents we needed: a passport for Lev, his visa, birth certificate, fees, inoculations, etc. Without Lena guiding me and translating for me, I would have been totally lost. Vladimir is a big city and difficult to navigate when you don't speak Russian. There are no English-language signs as there are in other European cities. We would take buses, trams, trolleys, taxis, and whatever it took to find the government offices we needed to go to. Offices were in some of the oddest places, such as apartment buildings. In every office we entered, we had to bring a gift in order to be served promptly and efficiently. Usually, candy or office supplies would work. They loved Post-it notes and paper clips. (There must be a shortage of such things there.) We went about for hours getting everything we needed before I would head off to Moscow. When we finished, we went back to the hotel. Lev desperately needed a haircut and new clothes to wear, as the clothes he left the orphanage in were pretty shabby. We went outside the hotel and walked down the street and behold a salon just a block from the hotel. We went in, and I asked them to give him a nice haircut, and they proceeded to wash and cut his hair. We also picked up some pants and shirts at a clothing store. One of my friends, Claire, who had just adopted the twins and their sister, had loaned me a heavy coat for him to wear until we got home. Once we were in Florida, we would not need a heavy winter coat. Now, he really looked handsome. We stayed at the hotel in Vladimir until it was time to go to Moscow and the American Embassy to get the final documents needed to enter the US. Jeanne made arrangements for us to stay at a hotel in Moscow that was just down the street from the US Embassy so we could walk there. It was required to go to the embassy once in the morning for an interview and return in the afternoon for a sealed package of documents that had to be turned in to Immigration and Naturalization in New York when we arrived.

On our last night in Vladimir, Jeanne had arranged for a driver to pick us up at four thirty in the morning and drive us to Moscow. I told Lev to get in bed because we would have a very early wake up. He didn't want to go to bed because he wanted to stay up and watch TV. With so much going on and so much to think about, my patience was running thin. In fact, I will have to say my head was spinning from all the things we had been doing and all we still had to do. I insisted that he go to bed and even went over and turned the TV off. This incensed him, and for the first time, we were angry with each other. He indicated that he didn't want to go to America. "No America!" he was shouting through tears. He started grabbing his few things to leave the hotel room and go out into the streets. I didn't know where he thought he was going to go. I grabbed him and pulled him back in the room and sat on the floor blocking the door. He kept yelling, "No America! No Fred!" I didn't know what to do. I felt like I had come to the end zone and now would not be able to go over the goal line for the touchdown. I prayed, "Lord, what should I do?" I felt him saying to me to call Pasha Baranov. I called Pasha and asked for his help. I told him Lev was yelling, "No America! No

Fred!" and kept trying to escape the hotel room. I was physically blocking the door and holding on to him so he wouldn't leave. If he escaped into the streets of Vladimir, that would be the end of our journey. Pasha asked to speak to Lev, and Lev got on the phone. I don't know what Pasha said to him, but he calmed down and got in the bed. I sat by the door the rest of the night, afraid that he would try and escape once I was asleep. Our relationship had always been so warm that this shocked me to my core. My spirit was telling me that Lev was simply afraid. He was afraid of what was before him. His life had been a simple one, living in Russia even in the orphanage. We had been up all day running from place to place to get his documents, and he was tired. Again, I prayed for about an hour. Praying that God would relieve any fear or anxiety on his part and replace it with the joy of a new future. I woke him up at four o'clock in the morning; he was pleasant as possible. It was as if the previous night had never happened. We were outside at four thirty in the morning waiting for our driver for the three-hour ride to Moscow. He never mentioned the fight the night before, and I never mentioned it again either. Somehow the Lord had gotten through to both of us and calmed our souls. Thank you, Pasha, Jeanne, Lena. How do people do this without such help? But we would still have to go through the chaos that was coming in Moscow.

CHAPTER 10

Moscow and McDonald's

We arrived at our hotel in Moscow at about seven thirty in the morning. Moscow is a huge beautiful city, but like all major cities, the traffic is impossible, and there are tons of people in the streets, stores, and many sights to see. I wanted Lev to know that he came from a beautiful and historic country. Since Lev had never been to Moscow before, I thought we would spend the day looking at sights, such as Red Square, GUM department store, the underground mall, and McDonald's. We went into historic churches and museums, but what impressed him most was McDonald's. Forget your ideas of US McDonald's. McDonald's in Moscow and St. Petersburg, Russia, are huge, with as many as thirty cashier lines and some multistoried. I ordered him a Big Mac. He absolutely loved it and asked for another one. He got another one, then asked for another. This boy was so skinny I could not figure out where he was putting them. He ate three Big Macs, along with fries and sodas, and I think he was still hungry. We finally finished up our sightseeing day and went back to the hotel. I called for a doctor to examine him as required by the embassy. The doctor came to the hotel room, examined him, gave him a few shots, and said he appeared healthy. He gave me a certificate of good health to give to the embassy. That evening, when I thought we were finished for the day, Lev asked if he could go out and get another Big Mac. I said, "I don't think so. I don't feel like any more walking." He would say, "Beeg Mac please." How we communicated, I'm not even sure, but he let me know in some way that he remembered where the store was, and he could go and return by himself. I just gave in, prayed, gave him some rubles, and told him to come right back. Traffic in Moscow is hellish. "Please don't get hit by a car," I pleaded. I don't think he understood what I said, but he could tell I was worried. About forty-five scary minutes later, he was back at the room with a bag containing a Big Mac and fries and a big smile on his face. I think he was more pleased that I trusted him to do this than he was with the food.

The next day, we went to the embassy as required. There was a long line of Russians waiting outside hoping to get a visa to the US. We didn't have to wait in this line as they had a separate entrance for US citizens. I was interviewed by an officer in the embassy and told to return after three o'clock in the afternoon to pick up our travel documents. At three o'clock in the afternoon, we went back and got our documents. They warned us not to open the package, as it was sealed and was only to be given to Immigration in New York and not to allow Russian Immigration officers to open it. Our flight was scheduled for the next day. I prayed, "Lord, please let me get through all this and make it to the plane tomorrow."

The next day, we took a taxi to Sheremetyevo Airport to board our flight to New York. Thankfully, the airport has signs in English along with Russian, and this makes it easy to navigate around the airport. Lev had never flown before and was quite nervous about the experience. I had all his documents along with mine. I had enough frequent flyer miles from flying to Russia so much that I was able to upgrade our tickets to first class. So Lev on his very first flight would be flying first class. When we started through security and immigration, the agent asked for my documents and the envelope. I gave him my passport and boarding pass, along with Lev's, but refused to give up the sealed envelope. He stared at me for a while and then said to go on through. We went through to the boarding area. Because we were traveling first class on Delta, we were able to go into the first class lounge and get a bite to eat. We had a couple of hours to wait, so we strolled through the duty-free shops. The Moscow's Sheremetyevo Airport has a huge duty-free area with great bargains. Finally, it was time to board. Lev had a window seat, and I was next to him. As the plane roared to life, he grabbed my arm. The flight attendants shut the main cabin door, and the Jetway was rolled back. The plane was pushed away from the terminal and started rolling slowly to its departure runway. As the engines revved up, Lev held my arm so tightly that I thought he was going to break my skin. I told him everything was okay as the plane hurried down the runway preparing to lift off. As we lifted off and the plane was gliding up to its cruising altitude, the pilot came on the intercom and said the weather was good, and we should arrive at John F. Kennedy Airport in New York City in eleven hours. He said it in Russian and English, so Lev understood what he said and looked at me, and we both laughed. He finally released my arm as the flight attendants busied themselves bringing us drinks and other snacks. I pulled up the monitor, and somehow Lev figured out how to play a game on it. Teenage boys, no matter what culture they come from and even if they have never seen a video game before (which he hadn't), can figure them out. All the way across northern Europe and the Atlantic, except when we were eating, that boy was glued to the TV and those video games. He was now so excited.

Arriving in New York was anticlimatic. After clearing customs, we were sent directly to the immigration office where they received the sealed envelope, took Lev's photo, fingerprinted him, and gave us a temporary green card until the real one arrived. Thanks to President Bill Clinton and the 2000 law on adoption of foreign nationals, Lev became a US citizen immediately upon touchdown in New York and didn't need a green card except for temporary identification until he got a US passport. Because he was considered a dual citizen, we had to follow Russian adoption laws for two years, which meant he had to be seen by an approved adoption agency every six months. The agency would then forward reports and photographs to the Russian Embassy in Washington, which then forwarded them to Vladimir.

Because of the time we spent in Immigration in New York, we missed our flight to Tampa, so we had to fly to Cincinnati, change planes, and then fly to Tampa. It was a very, very long day; and on the last flight, Lev fell sound asleep. We arrived in Tampa completely exhausted. On the drive from Tampa airport to my home, I thought of the many times I had pictured Lev sitting in the passenger seat of my car, and now here he was. After twenty long months of rejections, prayers, and tears, my son was finally home.

I took him into the house and showed him his room and bed. He took his clothes off and fell in the bed and was asleep in a minute. He slept until about nine o'clock in the morning and then woke up and came in my room with a big grin on his face. "America" was the first word out of his mouth. Yes, I said, "You are in America." I got up and showed him around the house and outside. What impressed him so much was the fact that it was warm outside, and the trees and plants were all green. We obviously left all the snow in Russia. I was trying to see our neighborhood through his eyes, and all of a sudden, I started appreciating things that I had previously taken for granted. The cleanliness of the streets, the manicured lawns, the manageable traffic, and lack of potholes. (Due to the snow, ice, and salt, Russia has numerous potholes in its streets.)

The biggest hurdle to overcome would be language. Even though Lev and I understood each other quite well through hand signals, some Russian on my part, and the use of our little computer translator, I knew he would have to learn English if he were to succeed. I had checked the school system out before I went back to Russia and found out that they have an ESOL (English for Speakers of Other Languages) in some of the schools. Because Lev was in eighth grade in Russia, I was told to enroll him in a middle school that had that program. The closest school to our home that had the ESOL program was John Hopkins Middle School. I let Lev stay with me for two weeks before taking him to the school. I took him to the school and let him see it and to meet his teachers. I could tell he was nervous and not at all comfortable. The next day when he was to start, he refused to go. He said, "No school." Again, I sensed he was afraid. I called the school and told them what was happening. They said they would have one of the Russian students enrolled there call Lev. A Russian student named Konstantin called Lev and encouraged him to come and said that he would stay with him while he was there. This seemed to satisfy Lev, and he agreed to go the next morning. I drove him to the school bus stop where he could get his bus to the school. He was afraid to get on the bus but finally did so after I promised him that Konstantin would meet him when he got off the bus. He and Konstantin became good friends.

Right after Lev started school, I had to go on a road trip with my job. We were doing training out in Colorado. How was I going to do this in the middle of trying to get Lev adjusted and not have him miss school? I called my son Chris, who was living up in Philadelphia, and asked him if he would be able to come down to Florida to stay with Lev until I returned, which would be a total of five days. He said he would come because he was eager to meet his new brother. The day he arrived was the day I had to leave. I was able to spend about fifteen minutes with them as they met each other for the first time.

Chris knew no Russian, so I showed him how to use the translator, and I was out the door to the airport. Things went really well at home, and when I came back, they had bonded. Wow. What a relief.

For the next couple of months, Lev went to school and seemed to enjoy it. The ESOL classes were great, and the teachers were awesome. However, it was the last couple of months of the school year. He graduated from John Hopkins and was assigned to Lakewood High School, where another ESOL program was in place.

We spent our first summer together bonding with each other and enjoying lots of activities in the area. Lev wanted a dog, so we went to the Pinellas County Animal Services and adopted a beautiful golden retriever named Honey. She was two years old and had previously belonged to a family that had been deported back to England for overstaying their visa. We took the dog home, and she was already housebroken with no apparent bad habits. Honey was a wonderful pet, and she reached the ripe old age of sixteen, became quite ill, and passed away in Lev's arms. Through the years she was with us, she was an incredible companion for Lev and me.

During the course of adoption, I was required to take a course on the problems of institutionalized children who are adopted. The course was on videotape. I listened to many horror stories about the problems many families encountered. Such problems included the children failing to bond with the adoptive parents, stealing, hoarding food, anger issues, etc. I didn't know what to expect with Lev. There seemed to be absolutely no problems with us bonding. He always called me Dad or Daddy. As he learned the words, he would express his love for me. He never stole or hoarded anything. The only thing I noticed was his frustration at not being able to freely express himself as he was learning English. We went to church each Sunday. Our church was sponsoring a camping trip for youth in North Carolina. There would be all kinds of fun activities, and I wanted him to go so he could get to know other kids at church better. He didn't want to go because he didn't want to leave me. I insisted he go, and when he boarded the bus, he gave a "look." When he came back and I picked him up at the church, he was all smiles. He had such a good time he wanted to go back to camp. He made friends and truly enjoyed himself. He showed me a picture of him in a boat going through river rapids with a huge smile on his face. This was the beginning of him getting to know other kids and to enjoy being around people other than me. His language was improving rapidly, and I found we didn't have to use the translator so much anymore. Since so many people had been praying for this adoption at our church, the pastor asked me to speak at the Wednesday evening service on the adoption, which I did. The story brought people to tears, with many—years later—telling me that was the most powerful testimony they had ever heard at church and an answer to prayer.

Lev has grown as a young man. A year after the adoption, we went back to Russia so he could visit his friends who were still in the orphanage and I could thank Nadezhda and so many others who helped us along the way. We stayed at a hotel in Vladimir. We went to Nadezhda's office and had an opportunity to thank her. She was overwhelmed with our visit. With tears in her eyes, she relayed how she was so thrilled to meet Lev. She told us that normally she only sees the parents and never gets to meet the children. She hugged Lev and asked him many questions about his experiences in America. I didn't understand much of what they were saying, but I could easily tell it was a wonderful conversation. Nadezhda also told me that she almost lost her job due to approving our case to go to the courts. However, she survived, and not only that but that it paved the way for other single persons to adopt in Russia. Lev and I were the first to be approved by a court.

Later, we were driven to the orphanage in the village of Lyahi so Lev could reunite with his friends. I was blown away by the reception he received by both the teachers and the kids. They were all over him, and he couldn't wipe the smile off his face. He took some of his closest friends to the store and bought things for them. We then walked over to the home of an elderly lady named Tamara whom Lev used to do work for—cutting logs, milking the goat, etc., for a meal. She was so happy to see him and made us come in so she could fix us dinner. Her home was very modest, but there was a real warmth and love. She even brought down an old bottle of champagne, which she was saving for a special occasion. Wow. I thought about what an incredible visit this has been. It was quite cold outside, but she had everything she needed in the kitchen to preserve heat. I couldn't quite figure it out, but there was some sort of fireplace built into the kitchen wall. It wasn't a traditional fireplace but a hole in the wall where the wood was placed. Once lighted, the entire wall would get warm and radiate heat into the room, but you couldn't see a fire. Strange but it worked. Lev wanted to take her to the store also. We went to the store, and she purchased everything she needed. Lev paid for everything out of his own money. I was moved by his generosity toward the kids and Tamara.

Back in Vladimir, we visited Pasha, Lena, Dima, and a host of folks we knew, especially Jeanne. What a gift from heaven she was. Without Jeanne, Pasha, and Lena, I don't think this adoption would have ever happened, or at least it would have been far more difficult. I believe God placed them in my life at the right time.

We went to Lev's apartment to see if we could meet the ladies who were renting it. We persuaded someone to let us into the building, and we went up to the third floor where the flat was and knocked on the door. A lady came to the door, and Lev told her who he was. She was obviously surprised, but she let us in and offered us tea. The flat was quite large by Russian standards (two bedrooms, a living room, kitchen, bathroom, and also three outdoor balconies). Lev shared with her how he used to live in the flat with his grandmother and how grand mom had a stroke and could no longer care for him.

At that point, the social workers came and took him to a children's home. The lady shared that she worked for the city of Vladimir and was renting the flat with another lady. The rent money was going into a bank account with Lev's name on it. We looked around the flat and saw that it needed quite a bit of work. She then showed us a bunch of boxes piled up. She said the boxes were Lev's grandmother's things that were in the flat when they moved in. Everything was still there—dishes, vases, sheets, pots, pictures, etc. We started taking down the boxes so Lev could see if there was anything he wanted to take back home. He saw some of his mother's wedding presents and wanted them. Also, he retrieved several photo albums with much of his young life played out in pictures. Looking at the pictures, his emotions welled up. He was thrilled to have pictures of his mother and other relatives and pictures of him growing up and in school. I asked Lev before we left if he would like to visit his biological father. He said no, I was the only father he needed.

On our nonstop flight from Moscow to Atlanta, we both felt a great sense of satisfaction at how well this trip went. No amount of money could have replaced this trip and the joy it brought to Lev and to me. We both came home at peace.

God is good. He knew that of all the children in the world, there was a young boy six thousand miles away in Russia who would be the perfect son for me. People sometimes ask me why I went all the way to Russia to adopt a (white) boy when there are so many (black) boys in the US in need of homes. In truth, my answer is that I did not go to Russia to adopt a child; in fact, I fought against it. It was God who answered my prayer for a son, and it was he who selected Lev to be my son. Lev is not my "white" son. He is simply my son, and I love him to death. After fourteen years, I can't imagine my life without him.

Looking back on the experience, I can see God's hand in every-thing that happened. During the time, I couldn't. It is almost like a jigsaw puzzle when you don't know what the final picture will look like. I didn't know how it would turn out; I just knew I had to continue to trust God. After going to Russia the first two times, I never planned to go back. But that was just God introducing me to Russia, a place I never wanted to go. In fact, I never wanted to go on a mission trip. Even on the third trip when I met Lev, I never once considered that he was the answer to my 1997 prayer. The truth is I never thought Lev was the answer to my prayer until it was all over and I was able to look back on it and connect all the dots. And believe me, the dots do connect—from the initial prayer, the trips to Russia, the rejections, to the judge approving the adoption five years later. I truly believe that God answered my prayer the second I prayed it when I left the courthouse in Clearwater. God worked out the entire plan, and all I had to do was not give up. God didn't have to think about what he was going to do. He didn't have to try and find a child as an answer to my prayer. He knew exactly which child would be the answer to my prayer. In all the world with hundreds of millions of children, he knew which child would be best suited to be my son. What a miracle. This was truly a journey of trust and faith. What an incredible blessing in my life.

Lev at six years old, while still living with his grandmother

CHAPTER 11

Lev's Story

At this point in my life, I have lived in the United States for fourteen years. I am a citizen of the US who appreciates in many ways more fully than native-born Americans all this country has to offer. My life in Russia was certainly different especially during the orphanage years. The years growing up as a little boy when my mother was alive and later when I went to live with my grandmother were filled with good memories. I was only four years old when my mother died, so my memories of her are limited. One sad memory I have of my mother was the morning I went into her room because she hadn't come to wake me up. On this morning, I went to her bed and called her, and she didn't answer. I kept saying, "Mommy, Mommy, wake up," and she didn't wake up. I went next door to our neighbor's flat and told her I couldn't wake Mommy up, and she came over and tried. Things then became a blur in my mind, and the next thing I knew, my grandma came in and said my mother had gone to heaven, and I would live with her from now on. Lots of people came in to our flat, and they brought a casket in and put Mom in it, and people looked at her and cried, and I cried. She was so young and pretty. She was not quite thirty years old. I never knew exactly what my mom died of but later was told it was kidney disease. The neighbors took my mom to the cemetery in the back of a truck, and she was buried. My dad had already left, and now my mom was with Jesus.

Living with my grandma was good even though I missed my mom very much. Grandma was strict with me, but I knew she loved me very much. My fondest memories revolve around getting on the train with my grandma and traveling out to our dacha to plant potatoes and other vegetables. When we picked the produce in the fall, it would last us all winter. People in Russia grow a lot of their own food for survival. Nobody has lawns to grow grass on. If they have such space, they use it to grow food.

I was about six or seven years old when my grandmother had a stroke and could no longer care for me. In fact, she could not even get out of bed. I remember people coming to my house and telling her they would have to take me away to live somewhere else. Not again. I was terrified and cried like a little baby to know that I would not be around my grandma. I wanted to take care of her, but they wouldn't let me. I was told I was too young. They took me to a children's home and told me that was where I was going to live. There were many kids there my age, but I hated it. I wanted to go home. I wanted to see Grand Mom, and I wanted to go to the dacha and pick potatoes. I wanted to go to my school in Vladimir. I was very sad. My mom had died; my grand mom was sick, and my dad didn't want me.

After a short several months, I was told that I would be moving to another children's home because they wanted to unite two brothers who were separated in different homes. That's when I was moved to Lyahi, a home in much worse condition than the first home.

I remember when my dad left, he yelled at my mom and told her that he didn't want to see her again, and he didn't want to see me. At that time, my mom was very ill and only about twenty-eight years old. Dad walked out, and I didn't see him again until ten years later when they took him to court to terminate his parental rights.

He never came to see me in the orphanage, and he never wrote me a letter or sent me a card on my birthday. He never bought me a gift. I don't wish him any ill. I know he has a new wife and other children whom I have never met. It's okay because I have a new life also. When Fred (my true dad) asked me when we were in Vladimir if I wanted to visit my biological dad, I said I did not because I saw nothing to be gained from such a visit. Not knowing if he even let his children know about me might have damaged his current relationship with his wife and children if they found out. So as they say, "Let sleeping dogs lie."

My life with my new family has been a dream come true. As I was growing up in the orphanage, I thought very little of my future. Other kids who left the orphanage at about sixteen or seventeen usually had pretty dismal lives. Boys ended up in the army, and many of the girls ended up in dead-end jobs in factories. Many of the kids went to jail for petty crimes. Without good education and a family to help, a life of crime seemed almost inevitable. Thank God that mission teams from America started coming to the orphanage and teaching us about Jesus. I remember giving my life to the Lord and getting baptized while in the orphanage. Jeanne, Dima, Pasha, Lena, and others coming to the orphanage to see that we knew about the Lord was the very thing that prevented me from going over the deep end at times. Pasha taught us the Bible. Dima taught us Christian songs, and all the rest of the missionaries from Russia and America just loved on us. I was not always a good little boy. In fact, I did things that I do regret, but they continued to love me. The summer I met Fred who was with a team from Calvary Chapel in Florida, I felt something click between us. We played ball, games, and did crafts; and it was great having a grown man in my life. Virtually, all the staff in orphanages are women. The boys had no other role models. The men on the teams took special time with the boys to help us grow into decent men.

During my last year in the orphanage, my grandma died. I was so heartbroken. She was the only relative I had left who truly loved me. By the time the staff got me back to Vladimir to attend her funeral, she had already been buried, so I never got a chance to say, "Good-bye, Grand Mom." After that, I didn't know what to do with myself. I just prayed and prayed that Fred would be able to adopt me. I knew that he was trying, but I didn't know what was happening, and it was torture. The other kids would tease me, and I would lash out at them, and then I would be punished and have to wash floors or clean the kitchen. I was truly heartsick not knowing.

One of the great times for me was when the team came back for the second summer camp and I was able to leave the camp for the weekend and spend it with Jeanne and Fred at Jeanne's flat in my hometown of Vladimir. I was able to show Fred where I lived with my grand mom and show him around the city. Vladimir is a really big city, but we lived right downtown, which was wonderful. My grand mom's flat was right across the street from the city's soccer stadium, and because the flat had balconies, we could watch the soccer games from the balcony. I had lots of friends in the building. When I went back with Fred to the building, I got to see some of my old friends. What a fantastic weekend. It made me forget about many of my sorrows. I didn't know at that time that I now owned that flat. My grandma left it to me, and the city of Vladimir was renting it to two of their employees and putting the rent money in escrow for me.

Going to court for the adoption proceeding was terrifying for me. I was so scared that the judge was going to say no. I understood everything that was being said although Fred was kind of lost because he was only getting a translated version. I sensed that the judge was not in our favor, and when he asked Fred about God, I got sick to my stomach. When the judge asked me what I planned to do if he denied the adoption, I didn't know what to say, so I just stumbled over some words. Fred had to tell me what I said later. The two days in that courtroom were two of the worst in my life until the judge said the adoption was approved.

I've probably never said this to Dad, but even though I tried to act happy, I was very scared of what was coming. I wanted to go to America, but at the same time, I was scared. I wanted to be adopted, but at the same time, I was scared. Fear was gripping me, and I think that may have been what was going on when Fred asked me to turn off the TV in the hotel room and get some sleep. I was a fourteen-year-old boy with so many things happening to me, and I was scared. I had never been out of Russia, and I had never been on a plane. I was leaving everything I knew. I was leaving everybody I knew and going into a whole new world.

Since coming to Florida, I have been so blessed. I have a great family and many friends. I am still friends with the twins, Sergei and Kostya, and their sister Natasha who were in the Russian orphanage with me. They live across the bay in Tampa, and we get together periodically. I attend a good church and have volunteered at times to work in the children's ministry. I have a wonderful girlfriend Tiffany, and her family treats me as though I am family. I have attended two years of college and have a good job with Habitat for Humanity. I look forward to the future in a way I never did when in Russia. I thank God for answering Fred's prayer request for a son in the way he did. Can you imagine God sending Fred about six thousand miles to adopt a child? It didn't make any sense, but it was the miracle that saved my life.

Because I was so blessed to escape the orphanage before President Putin and the Duma enacted laws making such adoptions by Americans illegal, I felt it very important to write a letter to the president. I wanted to help those kids trapped in the system who had Americans who wanted to adopt them. Here is what I wrote and sent:

Honorable Vladimir Putin
President, Russian Federation
The Kremlin
23, Illyinka Street
Moscow, 103132, Russia

Dear President Putin:

My name is Lev Ragsdale, formerly Lev Migalinski of Vladimir, Russia. As a result of missionaries coming from St. Petersburg, Florida, to my orphanage several times in the year 2000 through 2002, I had the opportunity to be adopted and brought to the United States along with five other children who were in the orphanage with me. I was twelve years old when I first learned that someone from that church group wanted to adopt me. I was so excited and happy, but it took almost two years before the adoption became a reality through the Russian courts. I can't imagine the heartache I would have felt if my adoption had been denied for reasons having nothing to do with the adoption itself.

My mother died when I was four years old. My father abandoned me at that time, and I was left in the care of my grandmother. When I was eight years old, my grandmother had a paralyzing stroke and could no longer care for me. I was taken to live in a children's home in Lyahi, Russia. Conditions in the home were very bad, and there were times when we had very little food to eat. Additionally, the home did not have showers or flush toilets for the over eighty children who lived there.

Sir, living in an orphanage is extremely difficult for the children. The only hope they have and hold on to is that someone will want to adopt them and give them a real home before they are expelled from the orphanage at around age sixteen. Since it appears that Russians rarely adopt orphans, it is usually people from outside Russia who do.

I am asking you, as the president of the Russian Federation, to reconsider your decision to prevent adoptions by American families. I understand that the bill has been passed and signed into law, but I also know that laws can be revoked with enough reason, and especially if it is the will of the president. I would also ask you to go to one of the orphanages, sit down with a child who was going to be adopted, and tell him or her as you look him or her in the eyes that it is best that they don't get adopted by the American families they were waiting on and that they will have to stay in the orphanage until they age out. Their heart will be broken and, hopefully, yours also. Adoption is their dream and hope.

Please, President Putin, don't punish the children because of laws in the United States that you disagree with. These orphans have suffered enough in their young lives and would like nothing more than to be welcomed into a wonderful family the way I was. If you let these children leave, I believe you will be truly blessed for your change of heart. I know what it is like not have a family that loves you, and I don't wish that on any other child. I thank God every day that I was fortunate enough to be adopted and given a real home in St. Petersburg, Florida.

I am doing very well in the United States. I am a student at St. Petersburg College and work part-time at a local supermarket.

I wish you well as you continue your job as president of the Russian Federation.

Respectfully,
Lev Frederick Ragsdale

I love my dad, and I know he loves me. We have a great father/son relationship. I can't imagine my life any other way. I am so thankful that he was faithful to God's calling in his life and never gave up no matter what was happening. Thank you, Dad, for waiting for the fat lady to sing.

Lev enjoying Saw Grass Park in St. Petersburg
Summer 2002

Lev at home in St. Petersburg with German exchange student Patrick

Lev on trip to New York City and atop the Empire State Building
Summer, 2003

Epilogue

This story began with my praying for a new son when my son Christopher and I were estranged due to the divorce. I had no idea how long the estrangement would last or if it would ever end. I felt that I had reached out to Chris multiple times but was rebuffed. However, prior to the adoption of Lev becoming a reality, Chris called me to say he was sorry for what had happened and wanted our relationship to be restored. I was happy for the restoration as any parent is when a child returns to the family. However, by this time, the adoption was in process, and there was no turning back on my end. Chris cheerfully coming to Florida to stay with Lev while I went on a business trip was a great time for them to get to know each other, especially since they were now brothers. Funny, Christopher, while growing up, used to say he would like to have a brother. Who knew this would be the way it would happen?

Through the years, Lev has adapted beautifully to life in the United States. He has continued his relationship with the Lord, attending church faithfully and being a light to some of the young children in the church by volunteering to work in the children's church on Sunday mornings.

He is a hard worker and put in twelve years working for Publix Supermarkets until recently leaving to pursue a better position at Habitat for Humanity. As his dad, I am very proud of him and the progress he has made especially considering the first fourteen years of his life. I pray that God will continue to work in his life as he moves into marriage and beyond.

As much as I never wanted to go on a mission trip and never wanted to go to Russia, God had other ideas and another plan for me. Over a few years, I ended up going to Russia ten times, being blessed to minister to the most beautiful children and my wonderful co-laborers. If I had been asked to list a hundred ways in which God would answer my prayer, this way would have never made the list. As you can probably surmise, I give God all the credit and the glory for this incredible blessing.

About the Author

I am currently retired from a career at the St. Petersburg College where I worked as a program manager in the National Terrorism Preparedness Institute. In that position I, and our training teams, traveled throughout the US and even outside of the US training law enforcement, military, medical and emergency personnel on how to respond to a terrorist attack or the release of a biological, chemical, or radiological weapon.

On my third mission trip with my church to Russia, I met my son in an orphanage where our mission team spent two weeks setting up summer camps for the children. I wanted to see him get out of the orphanage, so when I returned home, I asked several families if they would adopt him. They were sympathetic but felt since I knew him, I should do so. I didn't believe I was eligible, and I wasn't, since I was divorced and over the age where adoption would be considered. Initially, I was turned down flat by the Russian authorities, but I persevered through the journey. And finally, an absolute miracle occurred, and a Russian judge granted the petition to adopt. The amazing thing about my story is that at the time of my divorce, I asked God for another son, because my first son had stopped communicating with me. However, I had absolutely no idea how God would bring it about. The book is about how God brought it all together in the most amazing way.

CPSIA information can be obtained
at www.ICGtesting.com
Printed in the USA
BVOW07s1251270916

463439BV00013B/44/P

9 781633 382923